KILLING DEPRESSION

Exposing the lies of the enemy within

Toby Ray

Dedication

This book is dedicated to the greatest woman in the world, the love

of my life and mother of my children. Together we have been

through the "desert" and come out stronger. I'm so proud of you.

And to my beautiful daughters who have endured graciously. You

are all God's favorites, don't forget that.

Table of Contents

Endorsements – Tom Crandal   5

Introduction   7

Section 1 – Biblical Foundations

      Chapter 1 The Bible   17

Section 2 Our Identity In Christ

      Chapter 2 The New name   33

      Chapter 3 New Creation   49

      Chapter 4 The Heart Of God   69

Section 3 The origin of lies

      Chapter 5 The Origin Of Lies   89

Section 4 Overcoming Lies and Killing Depression

      Chapter 6 God Will Work With You   107

      Chapter 7 Performance Mentality   123

Chapter 8 Grace Yourself   137

Chapter 9 Dream Big   151

Chapter 10 Spirit Of Offense   163

Chapter 11 Thanksgiving and Praise   179

Endorsements

Walking in freedom with a renewed mind is not only possible, but the inheritance of every believer. In *Killing Depression* Toby speaks with a raw approach that will eradicate lies and align your mind, will, and emotions with the truth that will set you free. Get ready for a journey of eradicating lies and stepping into truth and freedom!

Tom Crandall
Youth Pastor//Young Saints
Bethel Church//Redding, CA

Introduction

I can remember all the way back to the fourth grade, and how hard it was to feel any significance at all. Trying to fit in to the many groups was impossible because I really didn't know who I was or where I belonged. I hung out with what was thought to be the most popular kids. My friend Brian was the biggest, strongest and best athlete around. No one messed with him. But I was the smallest kid, and to others that meant that I was just the tag along. I played sports, tried singing in the choir and even tried playing instruments. I remember enjoying the activities regardless of what I was doing, but never felt like I was a significant part of anything. There was always someone smarter, more talented, more athletic, or better looking. You name it, and I was always second best, at best. I was fighting for significance and didn't even realize it. Fast forward a few decades and you will find me all grown up, still dealing with the same feelings of insignificance and unworthiness. The problem is that I am a successful youth pastor, and high school coach. I have a wife and two beautiful God fearing daughters. It seems on the outside again that I am at the top but inside I am still always falling short of being the best.

I grew up in the church, learning the Bible and what God expected of me. I heard that God loved me and I believed it. I followed all the rules, well most of them, most of the time. While in high school I participated in the youth ministry, one that saw revival and went from 30 to 800 in a year and a half. We saw an average of 20 to 30 salvations every week. I have seen God move in mysterious and mighty ways. My leaders loved me and made me feel more than welcome; I was wanted. I went off to a Christian college and continued to study the Bible and learn God's word but still felt very little significance in life.

I was a typical young man growing up and feeling insignificant, but I was not depressed. I didn't even know what depression was. I had never met any depressed people. Life was good, and I enjoyed and looked forward to living every day. I was never depressed, never felt completely unwanted or unworthy. My parents loved me and cared for me well and gave me as much as they could. I was likable and had many friends, and life was good. Girls and sports were never a problem. I was an all-star in three sports when I was a teen and usually had a girlfriend. As I look back now, it was never really about caring for them (the girlfriends), having a girlfriend just made me feel better about myself. (Sorry for the brutal honesty but I was too shallow to know how to care for others). Then I met Shannon who is now my wife of 20+ years. What I didn't know until after we were engaged was that she suffered greatly from depression, fear and anxiety. She had ulcers from the age of thirteen. She put a smile on her face every day and acted as if life was great but inside was hurting severely, suffering from what the world would call a very low self-esteem, but she was depressed. I had never encountered a depressed person before in my life. I had no idea what it was or why anyone would be depressed. All I knew at the time is that I loved her and hated to see her feel the way that she did.

Since we were married back in 1993 we have overcome so many lies of the enemy, and conquered the battles that he has attacked us with. We have learned from the Word of God, from great Bible teachers, and from revelation, just how amazing God is and how powerful He has made us.

So this book is not just for the down and out depressed people, but for all who simply feel insignificant, or just want to walk in the power and authority in Christ. Although feelings of insignificance are a part of depression, there is a big difference from being depressed to simply feeling unworthy or insignificant. There is an answer, there is hope, and you are not destined to live in misery. You were destined to live victoriously and full of JOY.

All over the world in every tribe and in every culture from the young to the elderly, we battle for an Identity. To know **who we are**. To know what our purpose is. It doesn't matter what our background is or what faith we belong to. Most of us struggle to know **who we are** and why we exist.

Over the years as a youth pastor and lead pastor, God has taken me through the wilderness to show me just **WHO I AM**. It says in James that trials develop our faith. I should be the king of faith by now. I know **WHO I AM**! I have no doubts, no insecurities, no fear and no feelings of unworthiness or insignificance. God has shown me and convinced me of **WHO I AM**. Shannon has overcome all self-hatred, feelings of unworthiness and even depression. It is now my heart and passion to share with the world just what God thinks of us as individuals. It's all there in His Word, from the beginning to the end, from Genesis to Revelation. God has written us a love letter to show us what we mean to Him and what His plans and purposes are for us.

I don't just want to show you, I want to prove to you just **WHO YOU ARE**. I want to give you more than just some Truth, I want to give you truth that will set you free (John 8:32). I want to reveal to you truth that will set you free from the feelings of unworthiness, truth that will set you free from depression, oppression, worry, anxiety and fear. I want to show you just how God has proved His love for you, and will continue to do so until you get it. **You are** more than significant! **You are** a world changer! **You are** a powerful anointed Kingdom builder! **You are** royalty! **You are** a Son/Daughter of the living God! Your Heavenly Father, is absolutely in love with you! He thinks the world of you!

What does it mean that **you are** the righteousness of Christ? What does it mean that **you are** holy and set apart? Pure? Set free? Free from Sin? Redeemed? Supernatural? What did Jesus mean when He said that you would do the same miracles and even greater miracles than He did (John 14:12)? Did Jesus really mean it when He said that you too have power over the wind, the waves, the raging seas, and the demons and powers of our world?

Together we will look at the scriptures, the words of Jesus Himself, stories of God's children, some testimonies of modern day people that prove **WHO YOU ARE.** You will even be looking back to see how God is already working in your life. It is my hope and prayer that this book changes your life forever more. It is my belief that one by one we will eradicate self-doubt, inadequacy, fear, anxiety, loneliness, worry, sickness and disease. It is our aim, our sites are set, the crosshairs are locked in, we are killing depression.

Section 1

Biblical Foundations

The Bible

John 10:10b

My purpose is to give them a rich and satisfying life.

What was life originally designed to be like? What was God's original design for how mankind would live life? Were we designed to enjoy it? Were we designed to work hard and sweat? How did God design us to feel about ourselves? How did God design us to feel about others, about plants and animals, about nature? Have you ever stopped to think that maybe we are short sighted? If you are reading this book, your answer is probably, " yes." God is a good God and He created us to live a life full of joy, full of laughter, full of peace, full of hope, and full of love. I can envision a world where all mankind has that kind of life in mind. Can you imagine your own life being full of joy, laughter, peace and love? It is what God had in mind from the beginning.

Each of us sees the world through a unique lens. The home we grew up in, our local city culture, the type of church we were raised in or lack of church background, all have taught us how to view ourselves and how to view God. Believe it or not, one probably has a nice little box that one has put God into. What we have seen and heard has determined how big and what shape God's box should be. I hope I'm not bursting any bubbles or causing any offense when I say, your box needs to be destroyed. One cannot keep God in a box. It's impossible! His ways are higher than our ways and His thoughts are higher than our thoughts. Let's blow this box up so that we can discover more of God and learn more of His ways.

Let's make one thing clear before we read any further. The Bible is the Word of God. Everything we say or believe, any experience we have, must be backed and confirmed by the Word of God. My opinion means nothing without God's Word backing it up. Your opinion is meaningless if it does not line up with God's Word. I fully expect people from many denominations and backgrounds to read this and agree. As we look at the Word I ask you to keep an open mind. Not everything you've been taught is correct. I was taught the Word growing up in church but I wasn't always taught correctly. I was taught one thing and then shown something different. I was taught that there was freedom in Christ (which there is), but I was shown how to live in fear. I was taught not to judge others as the Word teaches, but I was shown how to judge according to righteous acts. I was taught to love my neighbor as myself, but I watched the church separate themselves as if they were better than the un-churched. We grow up and we are taught what to believe by our parents and those in authority around us. Sometimes it is in line with the scriptures and sometimes it's not. Culture changes on a regular basis. The loudest voice can sway a generation to something that the previous generation would have cringed at. But God's Word does not change. It is eternal and steadfast; it does not change.

2 Tim 3:16-17 All Scripture is inspired by God and is useful to teach us what is true and to make us realize what is wrong in our lives. It corrects us when we are wrong and teaches us to do what is right. 17. God uses it to prepare and equip his people to do every good work.

Ps 119:89 Your eternal word, O Lord, stands firm in heaven.

You can choose to agree with it or disagree, but again your opinion doesn't matter. It's like gravity – you can choose to agree with it and stay away from the edge of a big cliff, or you can challenge it and jump. Your opinion only matters if it lines up with the facts. It's not God's fault if you jump. We can't blame God when we disagree with His Word and something goes wrong. The first step to becoming or understanding who you really are, is to agree with the Word of God no matter what. If your experiences don't line up with it, find out why, but first realize there is something wrong. Think about it this way. We all have some different opinions and we can't all be right, right? So, we are probably miss-informed on more than one or many beliefs. Your feelings are real! Your feelings are powerful! The problem is your feelings follow your thinking and if your thinking is wrong, then your feelings, as real as they seem, are wrong as well. We see things from a certain perspective, but if our perspective is wrong, then our thinking is wrong and our emotions that follow will be wrong.

John 1:1 & 14 In the beginning the Word already existed. The Word was with God, and the Word was God. 14. So the Word became human and made his home among us. He was full of unfailing love and faithfulness. And we have seen his glory, the glory of the Father's one and only Son.

God sent His Son, who is the Word, who is Grace and Truth.

Therefore God = Jesus = the Word = Grace and Truth. That is where we must begin.

Isa 55:11 It is the same with my Word. I send it out, and it always produces fruit. It will accomplish all I want it to, and it will prosper everywhere I send it.

If God sent Jesus (John 1) and He sent the Word (Is 55) then Jesus is the Word. Jesus had to accomplish what God sent Him out to do before He could return. Since He did return (Acts 1:9), we know that He must have fully accomplished everything He was sent to do. Jesus was sent to accomplish many things, but we will only look at a couple for now. We will be looking into all these things until the day He returns again, but we will fall short of knowing completely until then (1 Cor 13).

One thing we know, Jesus was sent out to do was save the lost, it's what we call salvation; but there is so much more to that. So, let's move on to a little more of what Jesus was sent to do.

Ps 107:20 He sent out his word and healed them, snatching them from the door of death.

God sent Jesus to heal, and He did. Jesus healed the sick, gave sight to the blind, and even raised the dead.

Acts 10:38 And you know that God anointed Jesus of Nazareth with the Holy Spirit and with power. Then Jesus went around doing good and healing all who were oppressed by the devil, for God was with him.

Jesus went around doing good and healing because He was anointed with the Holy Spirit and power, and God was with Him. I want you to think about that for a second. Anyone can go around doing good things. "Doing" is one thing, it is an act, it is something we choose to do. But Jesus did more, He healed because He was full of power because He had the Holy Spirit. Now if you are a believer in Jesus, and you have confessed Him as Lord and Savior (Rom5:8) then you too have the same Holy Spirit that Jesus did. More on that later.

1 John 3:8 But when people keep on sinning, it shows that they belong to the devil, who has been sinning since the beginning. But the Son of God came to destroy the works of the devil.

Jesus was also sent to destroy the works of the enemy. The enemy is crafty but virtually powerless. He has one tactic and that is to lie and get you to look away from God. He has been lying to you

We empower what we believe

from the beginning doing his best to steal your identity. Jesus came to destroy the works of the devil, to give you back your identity that was stolen in the garden. In the garden, everything was perfect. Adam and Eve had a relationship with the Father (Papa) that had nothing hindering the perfection of love and mutual admiration. Adam and Eve were loved and knew it. They were significant and had value. They knew that life was good, they were good, God was with them and all was well. When they fell, it wasn't because Satan was powerful, they were simply deceived. Satan rationalized with Adam and Eve. Notice the word rational-lies. Lies that sound rational and good. It sounded so good. It sounded better than what God had said. It sounded like God was holding back on them, but He wasn't. The same thing is happening today. Satan is lying to you to get you to look away from God; to not trust Him; to get you to think you are all alone. You are not alone. Jesus paid the price for your sin because He desired to have a relationship with you. That's why He went to the cross. As a matter of fact, He wants to be with you much more than you want to be with Him. His love for you is powerful, it bought you back from the ownership of the enemy. Your identity was a sinner and you belonged to the devil. But you are no longer a sinner! You are now a saint! Jesus has saved you from your sin and now you belong to Him. You are a new creation! The Son of man came to destroy the works of the devil and He did just that. Now the devil has no power over you because you belong to Jesus. All the devil can do is lie to you and tempt you. **We empower what we believe**! If we believe that the devil has power, we will be in fear and thus he has control over us. If we know the truth, we will recognize his attempts to lie to us and cause fear, and we will instead be able to dance with joy in the Lord. Modern day movies make the devil and all his fallen angels look so mean and powerful and scary. For some reason, we love to be afraid so we watch shows that are a serious exaggeration of their power and we think that it is truth. I admit the devil is crafty. He roars like a lion so that we will fear him but really he is like a toothless mouse. He makes movies that make him out to be so much bigger than he really is. The truth is, he is a defeated foe who is hanging on to his last breath.

John 10:10 tells us that the enemy came to steal, kill, and destroy. Anything that has to do with death is attributed to his works including sickness and disease. The second half of that verse tells us that Jesus came to give life, and life more abundantly. Life abundantly starts here on earth, not just later in heaven. What does life more abundantly mean? What exactly did Jesus do for us here on earth?

*Gal 3:13 Christ **redeemed** us from the curse of the law by becoming a curse for us—for it is written, "Cursed is everyone who is hanged on a tree."*

What does it mean to be redeemed? Was it only my soul that was redeemed or was my body here on earth redeemed? If Jesus was sent to heal and all who came to Him were healed, then why is there still sickness? Why do we still have to deal with the common cold? Why do we have to deal with cancer? Are we missing something in the scriptures that are answers to these questions? Again, my experiences have to be proven by scriptures or they are meaningless. We will answer these questions in the coming chapters.

2 Peter 1:17-19 When he received honor and glory from God the Father. The voice from the majestic glory of God said to him, "This is my dearly loved Son, who brings me great joy." 18 We ourselves heard that voice from heaven when we were with him on the holy mountain. 19 Because of that experience, we have even greater confidence in the message proclaimed by the prophets. You must pay close attention to what they wrote, for their words are like a lamp shining in a dark place-until the Day dawns, and Christ the Morning Star shines in your hearts.

Peter, James and John heard the audible voice of God. Peter said that the voice made them even surer of what the prophets had said. It did not differ from the Word but it backed the Word of God that was written. You may hear voices and believe that it was God, but if it doesn't line up, then it must be done away with (Gal 1:8). We love to take our desires and attribute them to the Lord. I have had several people tell me that God told them to marry a specific person. I'm not saying God doesn't communicate with us and tell some to marry, but many times it is just our desire to be married and we are being impatient about it. The Scriptures are the highest authority. God gave us His Word so that we might get to know our Father in Heaven. We must desire to get to know Him personally, not just as a distant creator. Like Moses we do not want to simply know His acts (the things He has done), we want to know His ways (the way He thinks, who He is).

The Bible is broken into two parts the Old Testament and the New Testament. The Old Testament was written for the people of Israel before Christ was came to earth. It does not mean that we are not to look at it. But we must understand that even though

> **God gave us His Word so that we might get to know our Father in Heaven**

it was written for us it was not written to us.

2 Tim 2:15 Do your best to present yourself to God as one approved, a worker who has no need to be ashamed, rightly handling the word of truth.

We need to learn to look at scripture and know who, what, where, when and why it was written. The law was written to show man his depravity. It was not written for New Testament believers. With that being said, it's good for us to know the law because it does say something about God's heart. The basic principle is to learn what was written for you and what was written to you. The Old Testament is generally about the law and the New Testament is about God's grace. Since our identity is in Christ because of the grace of God there is no need for us to be considering the law at all. We are in a covenant of grace and we should understand that covenant governs relationships. The Old Testament spoke of the old covenant and thus the relationship that the people of ancient Israel had with God is no longer valid for us. And we are not to relate to God with a covenant that is not valid.

Heb 8:6-13 But now Jesus, our High Priest, has been given a ministry that is far superior to the old priesthood, for he is the one who mediates for us a far better covenant with God, based on better promises. 7 If the first covenant had been faultless, there would have been no need for a second covenant to replace it. 8 But when God found fault with the people, he said: "The day is coming, says the Lord, when I will make a new covenant with the people of Israel and Judah. 9 This covenant will not be like the one I made with their ancestors when

I took them by the hand and led them out of the land of Egypt. They did not remain faithful to my covenant, so I turned my back on them, says the Lord. 10 But this is the new covenant I will make with the people of Israel on that day, says the Lord: I will put my laws in their minds, and I will write them on their hearts. I will be their God, and they will be my people. 11 And they will not need to teach their neighbors, nor will they need to teach their relatives, saying, 'You should know the Lord.' For everyone, from the least to the greatest, will know me already. 12 And I will forgive their wickedness, and I will never again remember their sins." 13 When God speaks of a "new" covenant, it means he has made the first one obsolete. It is now out of date and will soon disappear.

I personally am so excited about this new covenant of grace because the old one was impossible. No one could have made it had God not sent Jesus.

Gal 3:11-14 *So it is clear that no one can be made right with God by trying to keep the law. For the Scriptures say, "It is through faith that a righteous person has life." 12 This way of faith is very different from the way of law, which says, "It is through obeying the law that a person has life." 13 But Christ has rescued us from the curse pronounced by the* *law. When he was hung on the cross, he took upon himself the curse*

for our wrongdoing. For it is written in the Scriptures, "Cursed is

everyone who is hung on a tree." 14 Through Christ Jesus, God has

blessed the Gentiles with the same blessing he promised to Abraham, so

that we who are believers might receive the promised Holy Spirit

through faith.

Why do you need to know this? If you don't understand that the law

is no longer in effect you will be performance minded thinking that

you will need to please God by what you do rather than just resting

in who you are and being a blessing to Him. You may even think that

you are more righteous than others because you sin less. You may

even believe that God is the problem when things don't go as

planned.

If I want to know **who I am,** then I must know who He is! Since my

identity is in Him it is imperative that I know Him. What does He

think of me? And how does He see me? What does my Father in

Heaven say about me? Who does He say that I am? These are all

great questions. Questions that we need the answers to. The

answers are in the Word of God.

Section 2

Our Identity In Christ

2 The New Name

Isa 62: 2,3

The nations will see your righteousness.

World leaders will be blinded by your glory.

And you will be given a new name

by the LORD's own mouth.

It's amazing to me how we can look at some people and think they

have it all together but deep down inside they are a complete mess.

Their mind and emotions are at war with their spirit and their spirit is losing the battle. When they are in public, their demeanor and candor is pleasant and seemingly joyful, so as a friend or acquaintance we would never think that they need some love and affection and deeper friendship. Sometimes it may be more obvious or at least noticeable, but most of the time it is invisible. Recently, an elderly gentleman who is a regular attender in a church, involved in the men's group, took classes, and while being discipled, took his own life. He had recently lost his job, which in hindsight we know had caused a severe depression. His family and friends knew of the situation, and they were loving and supportive. Even though those

> **The mind is a tricky thing. It is the place where we think we have it all together at one moment, and the next we realize we are lost**

closest to him knew of the situation, they were unaware of how deep the pain, fear, shame, and depression was.

As a father of two girls, and a veteran youth, and senior pastor, I truly have a heart for the fatherless (Just because a student has a father does not excuse them from the classification of fatherless generation). I have a student, a beautiful young lady, I will call Mary, who comes from a broken home. She has been part of the youth ministry for about three years. She has been to camps, retreats and a somewhat regular attender of our midweek youth services. Her parent(s), mom in this case does not attend very often, and I'm not sure where dad is. She is an adorable young lady whom I love whole heartedly. She is sweet and kind and her smile will light up a room. I am aware of a tough situation at home but maybe, not aware enough. I hadn't seen her in a few weeks or maybe even months until recently. When I hugged her and asked her where she had been, she sheepishly said that a lot of things had kept her away, including being in the hospital. I told her she is not allowed to be in the hospital without notifying me (as if I am that important), and that she should have called me and I would have sat by her side. Then I asked her why she was in the hospital. That's when she hit me with a brick right in the forehead, she said she had tried to take her own life. I grabbed on to her and hugged her for a long time and I did my best to let her know how much she is loved. If I were to admit it, I might have hugged her to convince myself that I had done all I needed to, and that this was not my fault. Why would anyone want to end their own life? I don't get it. When she told me this, I became extremely angry. Not at her. I became angry at the devil. This is his doing. This has his name all over it. It is a plan to steal kill and destroy a life, so it must be of the devil. Mike Bickle of IHOP Kansas City says, "Anything that is against love, is a work of the enemy."

The mind is a tricky thing. It is the place where we think we have it all together at one moment, and the next we realize we are lost. Many have called the mind a battlefield. We are told in Romans chapter 12, to renew our mind, and to be transformed by renewing it. This means that we have control of it to some degree, but we must learn to gain full control. **You do have control over your mind**. Yes, thoughts come that are unwanted, perverse, mean, violent, gross, and weird, but what we do with those thoughts is controllable. What we believe about God, our perception of who He is, has the largest impact on our thought life. How we perceive him determines our future. If we believe God is mean or vindictive then we will have little hope of joy or peace. On the other hand, if we believe He is loving and kind and that He wants great things for us, then we have great hope. God is good! He is loving and kind and generous and so much more, so we do have great hope. But we also need to realize that God has good thoughts about us.

Psalm 40:5 O LORD my God, you have performed many wonders for us. Your plans for us are too numerous to list. You have no equal. If I tried to recite all your wonderful deeds, I would never come to the end of them.

Jer 29:11 For I know the plans I have for you," says the LORD. "They are plans for good and not for disaster, to give you a future and a hope."

He has a good plan for us and He believes in us, which is more than proven when He sent His Son to lay down His life for us.

In Judges chapter 6 a young Jewish man/boy named Gideon had an encounter with God that transformed his life. The Midianites had basically enslaved Israelites and were making life miserable for them. The Israelites would plant, and harvest only to have the Midianites take their crops. So they were frustrated, probably hungry, and living in fear. So the story goes that he was standing in a winepress threshing wheat. Hiding so that the enemy could not take his food. An angel appeared to him and called him a mighty man of valor. This is one of those must-see movie scenes that we will get to watch on Heaven's Netflix one day. Here is a young man who is afraid, so afraid that he is in hiding, and an angel appears before him calling him a man of valor, a warrior. I can imagine the look on his face at that moment. Without a doubt, at this point he is even more afraid and very confused, and rightly so. From his perspective, there is no reason not to be afraid. The enemy has oppressed his whole community, those he looks up to are not helping, and now there is an angel standing in front of him talking to him.

What happened next must have been very powerful. The Angel calls him a mighty man of valor, something that he did not see in himself. Yet Gideon didn't hesitate to speak with authority to the angel after the angel had said that the Lord was with him.

Judges 6:13 "Please, sir, if the LORD is with us, why then has all this happened to us? And where are all his wonderful deeds that our fathers recounted to us, saying, 'Did not the LORD bring us up from Egypt?' But now the LORD has forsaken us and given us into the hand of Midian."

Although his response was negative and from the wrong perspective, it still was bold to even say. Gideon may not have seen himself as a man of valor, but he displayed it with his character.

Soon after, he and ten men, are sneaking off at night to break down the altar of Baal. They broke down the altar and cut down the Asherah pole standing next to it. The next day the people who worshipped the image at the altar, were looking to defend their god and sought to kill the person responsible. And of course they found out it was Gideon and came to punish and maybe even kill him. But Joash, Gideon's father stepped in and said, "let Baal defend himself and strike down the guilty party if he is truly a god." Then Joash re-names Gideon, Jarubbaal, which means, let Baal defend himself. This is kind of a nick-name Gideon was given. You see God saw the true character of Gideon that no one else could see. He knew what Gideon was made of, because He knew what He had created Gideon to be. He spoke into Gideon what he was created to be by calling him a mighty man of valor. In other words, God said, because you are a leader and

> **Pride is a funny thing because it exalts itself in the midst of its weakness.**

a warrior, because I have chosen you to lead my people out of captivity from the Midianites, I am renaming you, "the Lord is with you mighty man of Valor." As the story continues Gideon grows more and more courageous even though he is a timid young man in his own flesh.

Before we gave our life to Jesus, we were a person of Flesh but no Spirit. Our flesh is weak and timid and full of pride. Pride is a funny thing because it exalts itself in the midst of its weakness. Once we chose Jesus as our Lord and Savior we were filled with His Spirit. The Holy Spirit. The Spirit man is now alive and in charge. The old man of flesh is dead. We are a new creation which we will discuss further in the next chapter. The only problem is that the dead man of flesh wants to live again. The biggest problem is that the flesh man doesn't realize he is weak and powerless to survive because He is apart from Christ. It is a mind that only has worldly knowledge. Unfortunately, the flesh is the one we naturally let decide things; after all, he is the one that sees, hears, tastes and feels. It is the part of us that the enemy preys on (John 10:10a). Without a true knowledge of the power of our salvation and redemption, it is all we really have to go on. It is what we know, even if it is an inferior dead identity. The spirit man is the identity that Jesus came to give life and life more abundantly, as he stated in the same verse. The actual meaning of the phrase "life more abundantly" is life as God knows it. Depression, anxiety, worry stress, etc. is not how God knows life. God knows who we truly are, after all, He is the one who created us. He has a new name for all of us. God knows who we really are. Our old name may be what we are known as to those around us and even to ourselves, but God has a name that we just haven't learned how to pronounce yet. As we learn to listen to the Holy Spirit, we will not only hear how to pronounce it, but what it means. The meaning of the new name is who we really are. It is our real identity. It is the identity that has the mind of Christ. Did you know that you have the mind of Christ? What does that mean? How does He think?

1 Cor 2:16 For WHO HAS KNOWN THE MIND OF THE LORD, THAT HE WILL INSTRUCT HIM? But we have the mind of Christ.

Jesus thinks about the truth. He is Truth! He is the image of the loving Father. He thinks like the Father. He is love!

What others know me as, or what I think of myself apart from Christ is meaningless. What God knows me as is, who I really am. What God knows you as is who you really are. We may struggle with our identity at times because life can be difficult and the battles we face can cause fear or simply remind us of times of fear. That's when we stop thinking with the mind of Christ and revert back to the flesh man. It is as that point where we must choose which identity we want to be. Which identity is the real one?

The key word in all of this is CHOOSE! We get to choose which Identity we want to be at any given time. I can choose to believe what I want to believe but that doesn't make it truth. There is a great scene in the movie "Liar Liar" with Jim Carey where he is trying to lie and say that the pen is red but it writes in blue. In the movie, he is a lawyer that lies as easily as he breathes. His son's birthday wish is that his dad cannot lie for just one day. The son's wish comes true but his dad doesn't know why he cannot get his lips to produce a lie.

Just because we want to lie, it doesn't make it true. Just because we believe a lie, it doesn't make it true, but it does empower that weakness in our life. Imagine that there was a bank account with

> **God knows how strong you are and what your worth. Not only does God know what strength is inside you but he also informs the enemy that you will defeat him.**

your name on it that had a lot of money, but you didn't know you had it. You would go about life maybe struggling to pay bills, worried and stressed that you just won't have enough. The truth is you had more than enough, you just didn't know it. Our goal and responsibility is to learn the truth about God and about ourselves and accept what He did to change our identity. Once I know the truth about what and who God created me to be, then I need to believe in my new identity.

John 8:32 "And you will know the truth, and the truth will set you free."

That sounds so simple, but as I said earlier our old nature, our flesh man wants to live. Gideon believed the Lord and won a great battle not only for himself, but for all his people. He was the Valiant warrior that God called him. It's really about what you believe. Think about the implications in your life. The old nature has flaws, bitterness, loneliness, anger, it is malicious, jealous, and envious, and can be just downright nasty. The Spirit man, the true identity, is full of the Spirit of God, righteous, loving, and full of Grace. It's quite obvious which one we want to rule in our minds.

My encouragement to you is that you stop and realize that you are so much more valuable than you may think. Far beyond what you can dream or imagine is what God has planned for you and what you are worth. God knows how strong you are and what you are worth. Not only does God know what strength is inside you, but he also informs the enemy that you will defeat him. The enemy knows that you are a victorious warrior and he knows that he is defeated. The devil is such a bad sport. He knows he is defeated, but he doesn't want you to know it. He attacks you and lies to you and does what he can to make you feel helpless and hopeless even though he is the one that is hopeless.

Continuing in Gideon's story in Judges, Chapter 7, God tells Gideon to arise and go down against the enemies' camp, "for I have delivered them into your hands". God even encourages Gideon to go down and listen to what the enemy is saying. So Gideon sneaks into the enemies' camp late at night and he hears one of them telling another his dream. The dream, like most dreams is wild.

Judges 7:13 "a loaf of barley bread was tumbling into the camp of Midian, and it came to the tent and struck it so that it fell, and turned it upside down so that the tent lay flat."

Then Gideon hears the interpretation of the dream.

Judges 7:14 "Your dream can mean only one thing—God has given Gideon son of Joash, the Israelite, victory over Midian and all its allies!"

Even the enemy knew they were doomed. They knew Gideon's name and they knew it was Gideon that would destroy them. Gideon could have chosen to believe that he was still the fearful, timid guy hiding in the winepress, or he can choose to believe what God said about him. 1

The process of learning our new name is usually not a short, overnight revelation. It is a process of discovering truth. Gideon would have never been given a nick-name (jarub-baal) or a God-given new name had he not been under difficult circumstances. It is the difficult things in life that help us see who we really are. I heard a quote when I was a teen but I'm not sure who said it, "Christians are like tea bags, you never know what flavor they are until you drop them into hot water." If life was easy we would never have the opportunity to overcome. As we learn to trust that God is on our side, the process of overcoming becomes easier. As we learn the power we have in our true identity, and we learn to pronounce our new name, giant problems look more like the ant hills that they really are. It's all about perspective. From the mindset of the flesh man, the problem is huge and unsolvable because it is a mindset apart from Christ. But from the Spirit man, who has the mind of Christ and has learned the Truth, the problem is just a small cone in the middle of the road. Someone with authority just needs to move it. Mary, my student I spoke of earlier is a great woman of God. She is a powerful agent in the Kingdom of God and the enemy knows it. The enemy did his best to take her out of the game because even he knows how powerful she is. She may not know it yet, she may not be able to pronounce her God given name yet, but she is powerful!

You will face many trials and tribulations and as you conquer them one by one you begin to believe the identity that God has declared over you. You will learn how to pronounce the new name God has given you. God will affirm the gifts He has given you, open and close doors for you, give you prophetic words and revelation through the Holy Spirit. These will build your new identity and declare WHO YOU ARE.

We are about to embark on this journey of learning our new Identity and learning to pronounce our new name that God has given us. We are about to embark on a journey of learning the truth and how to eliminate the lies that we have been taught or caught. We are about to embark on a journey of learning to walk in the authority of Christ, the power of the Holy Spirit and the love of the Father all in one. You are a powerful man/woman of God. You may be hiding in a "winepress", but God is calling you into your true destiny, the destiny that He created you for and has planned for you since the beginning of time. It's time for the truth to set us free. It's time for us to come into agreement with the truth of who we are, powerful, anointed, loved, children of God. It's time to learn our new name!

Here are some scriptures that have declared who you already are. Start with these and let God confirm them in your heart.

John 1:12- I am God's Child

John 15:15- I am Christ's friend

1 Cor 6:20- I belong to God

Eph 1:1- I am a saint

Rom 8:1- I am free from condemnation

Phil 3:20- I am a Citizen of Heaven

John 15:16- I have been chosen by God to be successful in His Kingdom

1 Cor 3:16- I am a temple, God resides in me

2 Cor 6:1- I am a co-laborer with Jesus

Eph 2:20- I am God's workmanship

Phil 4:13- I can do all things through Christ

Rom 8:28- I know that all things work together for my good.

Col 2:10- I am complete in Christ

Eph 1:13- I am filled with the Holy Spirit as a seal of my redemption

3   New Creation

*2 Cor 5:17 Therefore, if anyone is in Christ, he is a **new***

***creation.** The old has passed away; behold, the new has*

come.

 I was in Costa Rica on a mission's trip and we had an afternoon to go sightseeing. We were taken to the rain forest high up in the mountains where we visited a butterfly sanctuary. There were so many different colors and shapes of the butterflies, but I was in amazement at the size of some of them. I think I can say without exaggerating that the wing span had to have been twelve inches or more. Maybe that's not very big where you are from, but for me that is three times the size of any that I had ever seen. I am not a scientist but I was reminded of my high school days and my biology class. That beautiful butterfly was once a caterpillar. A caterpillar went through a process called metamorphosis and came out something totally different. Something that crawls on its belly and inches his way along its path and let's face it, is not very attractive, became something that is beautiful and flies from one place to another. It was a caterpillar and then it was a butterfly! Scientist might even call it a new creation. This is something that scientist can explain as natural. It is not a supernatural act.

The term "new creation" is just as it sounds. Our natural minds don't grasp the concept because it is a supernatural act. You are a new creation, a new being. You have a new identity. You went from being a lost sinner to a child of God. You went from being homeless, living in the streets to a position of royalty in the house of God. That is a great deal for our natural minds to really understand. Paul wrote something that revealed God's heart for His children. It says that Christ died for all so that those who received His Love would no longer live for themselves. Instead we would be ambassadors for Jesus. We would now represent Jesus to the world. It's very difficult for a person to be an ambassador to people that he has previously known. Even Jesus had a hard time in the town where He grew up and declared that a prophet is not regarded well in his hometown. Therefore, becoming a new creation is an important factor in representing Jesus. I love walking into a new church as a guest speaker. No one knows me, I have a clean slate to share God's love and it's much easier to be a representative of Christ. The same goes if I go to a friend's house in another state where I do not know the people other than my friend. I can represent Christ without any one having any pretense of me. It is more difficult when I am with people I grew up with. They saw me as a child, acting like a child and they still think of me that way because it is how they knew me. Jesus made us into a new creation so that even when we are at home it is as if I am in a new crowd. Shannon (my wife) grew up in a small Christian school. From her perspective, it was more about obeying the laws of God than it was about loving God. Part of her depression was not understanding at the time what it means to be a new creation. She was under the impression that she had to be perfect in order to fit in. She had to not only be spiritually perfect but in every aspect of life; her grades, sports, with the boys, etc. There is no way outside of Christ that we can be perfect. There is no way that in the natural state, we can be even close. To try, even as a believer in Christ, is futile. The only way to "be" what Christ called us to "be", is for Christ to transform us supernaturally into a new creation. If one has received Jesus as Savior, that's exactly what Christ has done. He has transformed us supernaturally into His image spiritually. We were created in His image. Then we were transformed spiritually.

I have a friend, let's call her Eve; who grew up without Jesus. Her family was not a safe place for her and she grew up very quickly in what we might call street wisdom. Let's just say that she knew more about sex, drugs and rock and roll at the age of 14 than anyone should know in a lifetime. Living in a hotel with a drug addicted mom who brought men home for drugs and money, is not an environment where a child grows up feeling safe. She was wounded to say the least. Then she encountered Jesus! If you met her now, you would see Jesus. She is a new creation who represents Jesus as close to perfection as I've ever seen. Love pours out of her like a broken and overflowing dam. She loves Jesus and loves people and her joy is contagious. If you know Jesus, your joy should be contagious as well. If it is not, it will be after you finish reading this chapter.

On a scale of 1 to 10 (10 being perfect) how do you rate yourself in being righteous? Most believers raised in the church would score themselves very low. We were taught that there is none good, no not one (Ps 53:3), and that was so true. Did you catch that I said, "was"? Without Christ, none of us has any goodness in us. I have had people tell me that they are a good person but they have not surrendered their lives to Jesus. In Matt. 5 Jesus said, *"Blessed are the poor in spirit"*. The first thing we recognized is that we are not good and that's why we need a Savior. But that's where being a new creation comes into play. There is a supernatural act of God that takes place when we receive Christ as our Savior. Now you are the righteousness of Christ (Rom 3:22, 8:10, 1 Cor 1:30, 2 Pet 1:1). So, if you rated yourself anything less than a 10 you are not thinking of yourself like your Father in Heaven is. Our thoughts of ourselves need to be lined up with His thoughts. If I believe that I am not righteous, then I will have very limited power to overcome the enemy's lies. To say that I am not righteous is to call God either a liar or to believe that the work of the cross is insufficient. 2 Cor 10:5 tells us to take every thought captive to obey Christ. If I am thinking wrongly about myself then my thoughts and beliefs

> **If my thoughts about myself do not line up exactly with the way God thinks, then I need to exchange my thoughts**

about me need to change to agree with Him. Say this out loud; "I am Righteous!" Say it repeatedly until it becomes a belief deep down in your heart. It is the truth! It is not based on your sin nature; it is based on the finished work of Christ. You are not righteous because of your actions, you are righteous because Christ made you righteous, but **you are righteous!** The same goes for being holy. Jesus tells us to be holy for He is holy. But in that command, is the ability to be holy because He made you holy already? So, if you are already holy in His sight, then all we need to do is reside in that place of holiness which is simply in His presence. In other words, we need to learn to live according to our new position of holiness. When I agree that I am holy, the power of sin and temptation is diminished and no longer has any power over me. To be holy is to be set apart for Him (1Cor 3:17).

You are full of power! How much power? The same power that was in Jesus is now in you (Acts 1:8). You have authority over the wind and the waves and over all the demonic powers (Luke 10:19, Matt. 28:18). At the time I was learning this concept, I took my daughters to a lake where we rented a pedal boat to have some fun. Just as we were exiting the marina, the winds came up suddenly and directly at our faces, and made it very difficult to get anywhere. My two daughters were young and their legs were too short to reach the pedals so it was just my strength, and that was not enough. God reminded me that I had power over the wind, so I did what Jesus did and commanded it to stop. The wind laughed at me and blew harder, or that's what it felt like at least. I prayed, I believed and I commanded for what seemed like a long time. My daughters, full of faith at the ages of 9 and 10, told me to give up and that I was embarrassing myself. I prayed louder, commanded with more authority in my voice and still nothing. Then I imagined in my head that God had a giant bowl in His hand. I imagined Him placing the bowl over the lake as I commanded one last time, and the wind immediately stopped at my command. To be really honest, my girls and I were shocked that it worked. Soon I was feeling confident and powerful. So, after crossing the lake and taking a break, I put my girls in the boat all by themselves and told them to pedal back to the marina where we rented the boat. I told them not to worry, short legs and all, I was going to release the wind and it would blow them back. They believed me. I imagined God lifting the bowl as I commanded the wind to blow again, and it did. The wind blew hard and strong causing waves in the water just as before. They were blown in the direction of the marina and arrived there safely and on time.

I told this story to some students in a sermon, and of course some did not believe my story. They wanted to, but it seemed so unreal to stop the wind. One day on a mountain retreat with some high school students we faced a bitter cold wind. It was early in the morning and the wind was blowing downhill directly in our faces as we rode the lift up the mountain. A student sitting next to me, looked at me, and challenged me to stop the wind as I had done before. His challenge was half out of true hope and the other out of disbelief to prove that my previous story was not true. I accepted the challenge, but with a challenge of my own. I asked the other students on the chair to join me in praying and believing as we commanded the wind to stop. I had them speak to the wind out loud which was very uncomfortable at first for them. We realized that the only purpose was for our own comfort and warmth, but so was the disciples and

> Declare this with me, "I am the righteousness of Christ and I have every spiritual blessing because I am united with Christ."

Jesus in a boat. We prayed, and we commanded. And then we prayed some more and commanded. We told the wind that it could return in 3 days after we were done having fun. When we got on the chair the next trip up, it was still blowing, so we prayed again and this time the wind obeyed and ceased to blow. All three students were amazed that they had participated in stopping the wind. Coincidental, maybe! But three days later as we were loading the car for the trip home the winds came back, so did the cold chill that we had not had to endure.

Eph 1:3 *All praise to God, the Father of our Lord Jesus Christ, who has blessed us with every spiritual blessing in the heavenly realms because we are united with Christ.*

Declare this with me, "I am the righteousness of Christ and I have every spiritual blessing because I am united with Christ."

EVERY SPIRITUAL BLESSING. Only a new creation could have every spiritual blessing. Because I am a new creation I am highly favored by God. I am seated with Christ in the Heavenly realm (Eph 2:6). I am full of the Glory of God (John 17:22). I have spiritual gifts to help build the body of Christ and the Kingdom of God (1 Cor 12:7). In other words, I am (we, you are) valuable! You are a valuable commodity in the Kingdom of God. You are part of His team, part of His plan, and at this very moment regardless of how you feel, you are qualified to be whatever God needs you to be. You have every spiritual blessing.

Are you starting to see that this was not just a lazy statement by Jesus? He was declaring something over you and me. We are not the same as we were yesterday. We are not the same as the guy who was struggling in sin, trapped by the ways of the world, stuck in bondage to the addictions of our past. We have been redeemed, set free and made new. It was nothing we could have done on our own or even tried to do. Jesus did it for us at the cross. He took our guilt and shame and traded it for His righteousness. His life for ours. Jesus didn't die just so we could get to Heaven, it was so that He could have a relationship with us now. So that we could do what He originally planned with Adam and Eve in the garden, to reign on the earth. It was so that we could be His representatives here on earth. If you believe that Jesus only died so that you could get to Heaven, then you will remain trapped in your old life with guilt, shame, depression and powerlessness. Who wants that?

You are a new creation! But learning to operate in your new identity is a struggle because the only reference we have is our past. You know the one that was weak, lost, and hurting. In the movie, "The Bourne Identity", the main character had no recollection of who he was. The government had stripped his mind and made him into an assassin. His goal was simply to figure out who he was in his past. Our goal is to forget the past and learn who we have become in Christ. We keep looking back to who we were, thinking that is who we still are. The enemy wants us to keep looking back because he is afraid of our knowing our future. The devil is an egomaniac. We know that, because he tried to take on God in the first place, he must be dumb; but he knows enough to realize that if you figure out who you really are, you will be very dangerous to him. In the movie, the government didn't want Bourne to figure out who he was because he would be dangerous to them so they tried to have him killed. The enemy can't kill you, but he will do everything he can to persuade you to look back and stay where you are. He came to steal, kill, and destroy. Keeping you where you were, is as good as killing you. Not knowing our new identity keeps us powerless to do what God has called us to do. Think of it this way, you have been given all authority like a new police officer straight out of the academy. You even have a gun to enforce your authority. But if you don't know how to use the gun properly, it is not only useless, but dangerous. Practicing with the gun in a safe place is a good thing. Getting very familiar with the gun and understanding that it is only to be used for the purpose of enforcing legal authority is vital for you to be a successful officer of the law. As a new creation, you have been given all authority to trample on the enemy, to take back for the Kingdom what the enemy has stolen. We are commanded by Jesus to go into all the world and make disciples. I need that authority and I need to know how to enforce that authority if I expect to be a successful child of God. I have to know what authority I have because the enemy is crafty (dumb to go against God, but crafty) and will do his best to stop me.

The story I shared earlier where I commanded the wind to obey me is a perfect example on my having authority, but having to learn to enforce it with power. Jesus said if we had the faith of a mustard seed we could tell this mountain to be removed and thrown into the sea (Matt. 17:20, Luke 17:6). That would require faith and action. First the faith to believe what is naturally impossible, and second to put that faith into action. We

> **Not knowing our new identity keeps us powerless to do what God has called us to do.**

must act on what God tells us, if we expect God's Word to become a reality in our life. We can have wishful thinking but if we don't act, then nothing gets done. Let's say I see a man limping down the street as he walks. I believe God heals, so I pray silently for the man to be healed and then continue walking by. Did I put my faith into action or did I just hope that God would do something miraculous because I prayed? There is nothing wrong with praying for a stranger silently, it's a great place to start. But it is not what Christ compelled us to do. The truth is Jesus sent us out to heal the sick, raise the dead, cast out demons, etc. He didn't tell us to pray and ask Him to do it. He gave us authority and told us to use it. It is in our DNA as believers to have authority. It is part of who we now are as new creations. More on this topic later.

Eph 2:10 *For we are God's masterpiece. He has created us anew in Christ Jesus, so we can do the good things he planned for us long ago.* He created us anew, gave us a new identity and told us to be like Jesus. There is a reason for you have this new identity. He wants you on His team and He needs you. It was His plan from the beginning to partner with man. And from the moment Adam and Eve fell, it was His plan to redeem man, and to partner with man. It is only because of the new identity that we can be like Jesus. It is a gift from Him, but we must embrace the truth of who we now are so that we can operate in the way that Jesus did. Jesus planned for us to do good things long ago; but we keep trying to do them the way we used to and we continue to fail. When we do them from our new position, and new identity, only then will we begin to succeed. This is what Jesus meant when He said,

John 14:12 "I tell you the truth, anyone who believes in me will do the same works I have done, and even greater works, because I am going to be with the Father".

Now this new identity is taking on a whole new meaning. If we believe in Jesus we will do the same works that He did. Stop right there! Jesus healed the sick, gave sight to the blind, open the ears of the deaf and even raised the dead. Most importantly he gave life to those who were lost. To be like Jesus, we would have to be able to do those things. We would have to have supernatural power like He did! Wait! He said we would do even greater things. Is there anything that Jesus didn't do? How are we supposed to do greater things? This would require that we are "born again", "like Him", thus a new creation.

The one thing that is made clear is that this is a choice. When we decide to follow Jesus, we become a new creation, but we must choose to be that new creation.

Eph. 4:23 throw off your old sinful nature and your former way of life, which is corrupted by lust and deception. 23 Instead, let the Spirit renew your thoughts and attitudes. 24 Put on your new nature, created to be like God—truly righteous and holy.

We must allow the Spirit of God to help us renew our thoughts so that they line up with His. The old thoughts must be put away in a box and shipped off to a faraway land never to return. New thoughts, thoughts from God must replace the old. We must learn to take every thought captive to the obedience of Christ (2 Cor 10:5), and line them up with the thoughts that God has for us. We are a new creation, we are His creation, and we must renew our minds to be what He created us to be.

Paul says in Gal. 3:27 that we have put on Christ like putting on new clothes. And in Ephesians 4:24, he says that the new man gets put on. So, the new man gets put on like new clothes at the moment one puts on Christ. When we except Christ as our Savior, we are putting on Him. The new creation experience happens the moment we are saved. You are according to the Bible, Christ with skin. We are to re-present Him to the world. That means that when others see us, they see Christ in us. It is no longer you who live but Christ lives in you (Eph. 2:20).

Romans 12:1, 21- I appeal to you therefore, brothers, by the mercies of God, to present your bodies as a living sacrifice, holy and acceptable to God, which is your spiritual worship. ² Do not be conformed to this world, but be transformed by the renewal of your mind, that by testing you may discern what is the will of God, what is good and acceptable and perfect.

Transformation is only done by the renewing of the mind, which means we think differently than we did before, which is the definition of repentance. He told us to think differently so that our thoughts would line up with who we truly are in Him. By thinking like Jesus, and acting like Jesus, we prove what the will of God is to the rest of the world. "God's will", just doesn't happen automatically.

He works within us to see His will come to fruition. Let me give you a simple example. We know that it is God's will that all should be saved. But not all are saved are they? That's why He sent us out to help see "His will" happen.

Rom. 16:20 The God of peace will soon crush Satan under your feet...
Notice the term, "under your feet". In order for something to be under your feet, you have to take a step. God will crush Satan when you step!

Matt. 28:18 And Jesus came and said to them, "All authority in heaven and on earth has been given to me".
This is the beginning of a famous passage called the great commission. It is when Jesus gives us the commission to go. Before we look at the command we have to look at the word "all". If Jesus has all authority, then who else has any. The devil had authority until the cross and resurrection. Now Jesus has it all.

Matt 28: 29 "Go therefore and make disciples of all nations, baptizing them in the name of the Father and of the Son and of the Holy Spirit, 20 teaching them to observe all that I have commanded you. And behold, I am with you always, to the end of the age."

So, with all authority Jesus commanded His disciples (us) to go and make disciples. But the key is in His last statement, "I am with you always even to the end of the age". Because Jesus is with you, actually in you and working through you, because you re-present Jesus and have the same Holy Spirit living within, you actually carry the same authority Jesus did.

John *20:21 Jesus said to them again, "Peace be with you. As the Father has sent me, even so I am sending you."*

We are being sent the same way Jesus was sent by His Father. We aren't being sent with less! "As Jesus was sent", means with the same authority and ability. Whatever it was that Jesus was sent with, you have it too.

2 Cor. 1:20 *For all of God's promises have been fulfilled in Christ with a resounding "Yes!" And through Christ, our "Amen" (which means "Yes") ascends to God for his glory.*

All the promises of God are yes and amen for you. It is your inheritance as a child of God, it is part of who you are. If your parents left you a large sum of money, would you lay claim to it? What if someone came and claimed that your parents didn't mean it and that the money was to go somewhere else? You have it in writing in the Will. It is signed with ink and nothing can change it. It is yours, even if someone tries to tell you otherwise. You are a new creation! You are the righteousness of Christ and you have all the authority of heaven backing you. Lay claim to it and be what God has created you to be. The new creation understands that we are on the winning side. We are on God's team. We are filled with righteousness, peace and Joy. Don't stop! When you are constantly filled with righteousness, peace and joy, you will know that your thoughts are lining up with God's and that's where we want to be.

4   The Heart of God

John 1:18

*No one has ever seen **God**. But the unique One, who is himself **God**, is near to the Father's **heart**. He has revealed **God** to us*

The Bible as we know is a love letter from God to His children. It has so much in it that we will be forever discovering new things about Him and His ways. As a pastor one of the most common questions I hear is, "what is God's will for my life?" Well, to understand God's will for your life, first you must understand God's heart, not just what He does but who He is. Then you can go further and get a glimpse of your life in specific terms.

Let's look at God's "will" in general first. Let's start by asking, what is God's heart? Why were we created?

1 Tim 2:3-4, this is good and pleases God our Savior, 4. who wants everyone to be saved and to understand the truth.

We know God wants everyone to be saved. The most famous verse out of the whole Bible reads,

John 3:16-17 "For God loved the world so much that he gave his one and only Son, so that everyone who believes in him will not perish but have eternal life. 17, *God sent his Son into the world not to judge the world, but to save the world through Him*".

> **If our experiences don't line up with the Word, then our opinion means nothing.**

It is safe to say that God wants to save everyone. He loves His children and wants them to understand His love and receive Him. It doesn't matter the depth of their rebellion, time, location, or anything else, God wants them saved. Now what about this question, does God want everyone to be healed? I have heard so many answers to this question it's mind boggling. Based on our experiences we would have to say NO! We have seen death before its time in sickness, disease, accidents, and murder. If God wanted all to be healed, then no one would ever die, right? Well, remember I said at the beginning that the Word of God must come before our experiences. If our experiences don't line up with the Word, then our opinion means nothing.

I'm going to show you that God wants everyone to be healed just like he wants everyone to be saved. Let's look back to a famous Old Testament prophecy about Jesus.

Isa. 53:4-5 Yet it was our <u>weaknesses</u> He carried; it was our <u>sorrows</u> that weighed Him down. And we though his troubles were a punishment from God, a punishment for his own sins! 5. But He was pierced for our rebellion, crushed for our sins. He was beaten so we could be whole. He was whipped so we could be <u>healed.</u>

The first part of this verse in this translation uses the word *weaknesses*. Other translations use the word *"griefs"*. The funny thing about translation is that many words could have been used so they, the translators, chose the one they thought was best suited for the specific use. The other words that could have been used are sickness, disease, anxiety, infirmity and others. Then "sorrows" could have been replaced with anguish, affliction, or pain. Both words used in the Hebrew are more often used when referring to physical pain or physical infirmities, but they could also include emotional pain.

By His stripes, WE ARE HEALED. Okay, so now we must ask what this means. What does "healed" really mean? Is it just our soul that is healed or is it our physical bodies, and if so, to what degree? The only way to answer questions like these is to look at the words of Jesus Himself, and to prophecies that was spoken about Him.

Matt. 8:16-17 That evening many demon-possessed people were brought to Jesus. He cast out the evil spirits with a simple command, and he healed all the sick. 17. This fulfilled the word of the Lord through the prophet Isaiah, who said, "He took our sicknesses and removed our diseases."

Matthew quotes prophecy in Isaiah using the correct terminology saying he took and removed. Jesus healed physical people of physical sicknesses and cast out demons to fulfill prophecy. The curious thing is, He had not been whipped at the whipping post yet.

The actual fulfillment of prophesy was Jesus being beaten at the whipping post and receiving the stripes across his back.

1 Peter 2:24 He personally carried our sins in His body on the cross so that we can be dead to sin and live for what is right. By His wounds, you are healed.

This verse is in reference to the same prophecy. Jesus bore our sins and the punishment for us so we don't have to.

There are two parts to the atonement. The beating at the whipping post was the first part where the Body of Jesus was broken for us, providing us with physical healing (1 Pet 2:24), which is the bread of Communion. The second part is the death on the cross which we know was the shedding of His blood for the

> **If we don't doubt that God wants to save someone than we should not doubt that God wants to heal as well.**

remission of our sins and the establishment of the new covenant (Rom 5:8) which is the wine of Communion. If healing is already provided for, then why are we not already healed? Why do good people get cancer and even a cold or a flu? Well if salvation is already provided for, then why are not all already saved? God's will

is for all mankind to be saved and to be healed. Just like salvation

takes faith, so does our healing.

Some reason that one is not healed because God is sovereign and can

do what He wants. If that's the case, then we must question

salvation? If we reason that someone is not healed because of God's

timing, then how sure are we that we are saved and God doesn't

have a different time picked for one to be saved? Everything you

believe about salvation should be in line with what you believe about

healing, because they were both provided for at the atonement. If

we don't doubt that God wants to save someone, then we should not

doubt that God wants to heal as well. The only biblical example that

some use to refute this, is the story in 2 Corinthians about Paul.

2 Cor. 12:7, So to keep me from becoming conceited because of the

surpassing greatness of the revelations, for this reason, to keep me

from exalting myself, there was given me a thorn in the flesh,

a messenger of Satan to torment me—to keep me from exalting

myself! 8 Concerning this I implored the Lord three times that it might

leave me. 9 And He has said to me, "My grace is sufficient for you, for power is perfected in weakness." Most gladly, therefore, I will

rather boast about my weaknesses, so that the power of Christ may

dwell in me. 10 Therefore I am well content with weaknesses, with

insults, with distresses, with persecutions, with difficulties, for Christ's

sake; for when I am weak, then I am strong.

There is no mention of a sickness in this passage. It is a guess at best

to try and describe Paul's "thorn in the flesh". Some say he had

horrible eyesight because when he faced the high priest, he did not

recognize him. All we know for sure is that it was a messenger of

Satan. A messenger relays messages. It could have been guilt from

his past as he had persecuted Christians before his conversion. Or it

could have been his wife. Before his conversion, Paul was a rising

member of the Sanhedrin.   One of the requirements would have

been that he was married. Because there is no mention in the Bible

about his wife, some reason that she was his "thorn". Yes God

allowed the "thorn in the flesh" to stay because it kept him from

exalting himself. Paul was a leading Pharisee, full of pride, and had

exalted himself above all gentiles and even God's chosen people. The

Pharisees were the religious leaders that taught the Law, (lawyers)

as well as convicting others of their sin, (priest), in their mind they were high and above all those sinners (Luke 18:11).

Mark 2:3-12 Four men arrived carrying a paralyzed man on a mat. 4. They couldn't bring him to Jesus because of the crowd, so they dug a hole through the roof above his head. Then they lowered the man on his mat, right down in front of Jesus. 5. Seeing their faith, Jesus said to the paralyzed man, "My child, your sins are forgiven." 6. But some of the teachers of religious law who were sitting there thought to themselves, 7. "What is he saying? This is blasphemy! Only God can forgive sins!" 8. Jesus knew immediately what they were thinking, so he asked them, "Why do you question this in your hearts? 9. Is it easier to say to the paralyzed man 'Your sins are forgiven,' or 'Stand up, pick up your mat, and walk'? 10. So I will prove to you that the Son of Man has the authority on earth to forgive sins." Then Jesus turned to the paralyzed man and said, 11. "Stand up, pick up your mat, and go home!" 12. And the man jumped up, grabbed his mat, and walked out through the stunned onlookers. They were all amazed and praised God, exclaiming, "We've never seen anything like this before!"

Even out of the mouth of Jesus, healing and salvation are one and the same. Healing is to serve as a sign that God forgives. If they were different, then you could not use healing as a sign. Healing and salvation are one and the same but that doesn't mean that if you are sick or you don't get healed that you are not saved. The father of lies will try to convince you that you are not saved, that you are stuck in some sin or that you are not worthy for God to heal. Don't listen to those lies or even entertain those thoughts. Healing proves God's will for salvation not salvation itself.

Let's look deeper into communion and what it represents. But

> **Healing is to serve as a sign that God forgives**

before we do let's look at what happened to the Israelites the night after they took Passover for the first time.

Ps 105:37 The Lord brought his people out of Egypt, loaded with silver and gold; and not one among the tribes of Israel even stumbled.

God brought the whole of Israel out from Egypt and they were all healthy. How is it that approximately 3 million Israelite slaves living in the worst conditions in Egypt did not have one sick or weak person among them? The Passover that was ordained for them was to eat unleavened bread and place blood on the doorpost. Let me add that not only did they all get healed but they all became wealthy at the same time. It says they were loaded with silver and gold. Now, they had nowhere to spend it in the desert, they used it to build the tabernacle (it's all His and is to be used for His glory). My point is that God restored for them even the material needs. I want to add that we are not slaves to poverty because we are believers. (For a complete look at this topic may I suggest that you read, "The Supernatural Ways of Royalty," by Kris Vallotton). God wants us to have enough to share. How can we build his kingdom and support the ministry if we barely have enough to survive?

Communion is a significant part of our identity in Christ. If we read 1 Cor. 11 closely we see how we are supposed to take communion according to what it represents. It tells us to examine ourselves before taking the elements. Some would have you look to your sin and repent all over again as if God has all of a sudden remembered your sin that He separated from you long ago and forgot about. When we truly

When we truly examine ourselves, we are to remember who we are and whose we are.

examine ourselves, we are to remember who we are and whose we are. We are His children, we are redeemed by Christ and it is no longer we who live, but Christ who lives in us (Gal. 2:20). Verse 29 says that if we eat or drink without honoring the body of Christ then we are bringing God's judgment on ourselves. And then it says, *that is why many of you are weak and sick and some have even died.* Let me break this down as I have come to understand this. I am a child of God, fully redeemed and fully healed and yes fully saved. But if I do not recognize my true position as a son, then I think I must repent all over again or perform, thus nullifying the work of Jesus on the cross. If I am still trying to perform (working to access the benefits of the cross), then I might get weak or sick or even die before my appointed time. Trying to perform to be in God's grace is to deny the work of the cross. It is to deny the healing power of the stripes that Jesus bore. In other words, communion is an ordinance of God that was design to remind us of who we are and whose we are. I am saved by grace, it is not of my own, but it is the finished work of Christ.

The bread represents the body that was broken for us. He was broken, wounded for our healing. Bread symbolically refers to healing. Let me show you.

Matt. 15:22-28, A Gentile woman who lived there came to him, pleading, "Have mercy on me, O Lord, Son of David! For my daughter is possessed by a demon that torments her severely." 23 But Jesus gave her no reply, not even a word. Then his disciples urged him to send her away. "Tell her to go away", they said. "She is bothering us with all her begging." 24 Then Jesus said to the woman, "I was sent only to help God's lost sheep-the people of Israel." 25 But she came and worshiped him, pleading again, "Lord, help me!" 26 Jesus responded, "It isn't right to take food from the children and throw it to the dogs." 27 She replied, "That's true, Lord, but even dogs are allowed to eat the scraps that fall beneath their masters' table." 28 "Dear woman," Jesus said to her, "your faith is great. Your request is granted." And her daughter was instantly healed.

The woman came for deliverance from the demonic oppression of her daughter. Jesus referred to that (*deliverance*), as the children's bread. Bread is a staple food for children. It is what God used to feed the Israelites in the desert. It is a common daily necessity. When she responded in faith, her daughter was healed or delivered from that very moment.

John 6:32-35 Jesus said, "I tell you the truth, Moses didn't give you bread from heaven. My Father did. And now he offers you the true bread from heaven. 33 The true bread of God is the one who comes down from heaven and gives life to the world." 34 "Sir," they said, "give us that bread every day." 35 Jesus replied, "I am the bread of life. Whoever comes to me will never be hungry again. Whoever believes in me will never be thirsty.

Jesus declares that He is the bread of life. The reference to Moses was a reference to the Law, and that there is no life in the law. There is only life in Christ.

John 6:51, *I am the living bread that came down from heaven. Anyone who eats this bread will live forever; and this bread, which I will offer so the world may live, is my flesh."*

Now this is where it got weird for the many that followed Jesus. What did He mean they had to eat his flesh in order to live? Many at this point chose not to follow him because they did not understand the symbolism. His body, the bread, is symbolic for our healing.

Matt. 6:11, *Give us today our daily bread...*

Jesus is the bread and the bread refers to healing, and Jesus tells us to ask for it daily. Salvation is a one-time event that the enemy can't steal from you. We know that Satan came to steal kill and destroy. But he cannot take salvation from you. Nothing will separate you from the love of God. But healing is required daily, why? Because the enemy is always looking for a way to slow the children of God down from fulfilling the kingdom work. We are to look to Jesus and His finished work daily for our healing until we receive our glorified bodies. Healing, like food, is something our bodies need every day.

Rom. 1:16, *For I am not ashamed of this Good News about Christ. It is the power of God at work, <u>saving</u> everyone who believes-the Jew first and also the Gentile.*

The good news that we proclaim as Christians is not just that one day we can go to heaven. The power of God that is at work to save, is also at work to heal, to deliver, to set free, to make whole and to protect. The word used in the Greek in Romans 1:16 for *saved* is *soteria*, it can be translated many ways, saved, set free, redeemed, healed, or made whole..

1 Tim. 2:3-4, This is good and pleases God our Savior, 4 Who wants everyone to be saved and to understand the truth. The word used in this passage that is translated as *saved* is the word, *sozo*. It means all the same things as *soteria*, but you could add, *to do well* or *to preserve,* to the list of meanings. So it is God's will that all should be saved and all should be healed. Salvation and healing go together.

*Ps. 103:1-10, Let all that I am praise the Lord; with my whole heart, I will praise His holy name. 2 Let all that I am praise the Lord; may I never forget the good things He does for me. 3 **He forgives all my sins and heals all my diseases**. 4 He redeems me from death and crowns me with love and tender mercies. 5 He fills my life with good things. My youth is renewed like the eagles! 6 The Lord gives righteousness and justice to all who are treated unfairly. 7 He revealed his character to Moses and his deeds to the people of Israel. 8 The Lord is compassionate and merciful, slow to get angry and filled with unfailing* *love. 9 He will not constantly accuse us, nor remain angry forever. 10*

He does not punish us for all our sins; he does not deal harshly with us,

as we deserve.

What an amazing God we serve. He provided a way for us to be healed spiritually. We have salvation through His death and resurrection. But that's not all, He was beaten and bruised so that our physical bodies could be healed form head to toe. Sickness and disease are because of sin, but Christ has redeemed us from all the power of sin. We are no longer bound to sin and the sickness that came with it.

Even emotional sicknesses like depression. God does not want anyone to be depressed. It is not His Will that any should be even slightly under the weather in any way. Hopelessness, resentment, envy, jealously, laziness, and striving are all what we could describe as

> **God does not want anyone to be depressed**

something that interferes with love. It interferes with hope, and therefore it is not of God. We know that Jeremiah the prophet told us that God's plan for you is amazing, too wonderful for words. Plans to prosper you, to give you a great future with excess of hope. Yes, we will face trials and hardships, but we have been told to hold on to our faith because we know that these things are temporary and they will produce in us perseverance and strength, making us more like Jesus. That gives us great hope. If you are sick, physically or emotionally, there is hope. God doesn't just want you well, he wants you full of joy, full of life, full of Him.

Section 3

The Origin of Lies

5   Origin of Lies

John 8:44

*For you are the children of your **father** the devil, and you love to do the evil things he does. He was a murderer from the beginning. He has always hated the truth, because there is no truth in him. When he **lies**, it is consistent with his character; for he is a liar and the **father** of **lies**.*

Fear Vs. The Prince of Peace

By Mackenzie Hudgins

The voice of fear tried to convince me
I was safe because I was aware of threats
The voice of fear screamed so loudly,
That it would keep me safe, while all along,
Fear was trying to partner me with death.
The voice of fear tried to convince me
That peace is naïve.
It tried to tell me to stay quiet,
Because if someone heard me speak, they'd reject me.
It tried to tell me to hide,
Because if someone saw me, for who I am truly, they wouldn't want me.
It tried to tell me to stay small
Because if I got too big, I'd bulldoze the people around me.
If I got too big, I'd be too much.
The voice of fear kept me busy,
Day in and day out,
the voice of fear squawked and squealed, and barked and howled
It tried to tell me to shut down, stay quiet, don't fail, and don't sweat.
If people knew how hard you tried, they would know you're a fake.
You can't do anything right, you're a failure if you make a mistake.
Don't talk too much, you overpower when you speak,
But people like you when you are quiet, in fact, even better if you're
silent.
The voice of fear tried to teach me
Comparison is the only way to win, because in this game of life, it's
always competition.
Fear pointed at the mirror and showed me how I never measured up,
It robbed me of my security and put it in other things,
I listened extra carefully for any voice of affirmation,
Because if someone could tell me I measured up,
then surely, I was enough, surely then I'd be loved.
It convinced me to build up these walls of isolation,
Until one day, I realized I had built for myself, my own prison.
Locked up, alone, and somehow fear convinced me it was safe
Safer not to feel, safer to hide, safer to let everything inside of me
slowly wither up and die,
But the voice of fear is a LIAR.

See somewhere along the way, fear told me I'd be safe,

It convinced me that peace was naïve,
But one day, I met a bigger King;
He told me that I was enough, I didn't have to do a thing,
He told me how much He loves it when I speak,
He asked me to keep on talking because he loves what I have to say,
He showed me how fear was all just empty threats,
And this King, can only give me life, because He already conquered death.
This King told me how much I needed to be seen,
So He made me a light amongst darkness, so I cannot be missed, mistaken, or hidden.
He showed me how I was made for bigger things,
How I needed to dream bigger, because He does all sorts of impossibilities.
He told me that the bigger I got, the higher I could lift up people all around me.
This King taught me to stop striving, because it was like riding on a stationary bike and expecting to get somewhere,
Instead he showed me how resting positioned me for exponential increase, because it allowed Him to be King, and me to be me.
He told me to stand up, to speak, to be okay with process, and to dream.
If people saw me stand up, soon they too would rise,
And when I speak, people begin to come back to life
That process never disqualifies,
Dreaming brings heaven into reality.
This King taught me, that life is meant to be in community,
That as a body, everyone gets to play their part, and one part without the other, and we all fall apart.
He told me I was loved, and for some reason that was enough,
He invited me into family,
A place where when I succeeded, I was celebrated,
And where I failed, I was accepted.
He invited me into peace,
And for the first time, I felt security.
He is the prince of Peace,
And the voice of fear is a liar.

One of the great things about getting married is the honeymoon. Many young people dream of the perfect vacation spot to spend some time with their new spouse. Some love the mountains and the snow, but most dream of a place in the warm sand and sunshine where others are waiting on them hand and foot. Some friends of mine went to such a place with excitement and expectation. When they arrived at the hotel, there was a mix-up in the reservations and there were no rooms available. They were not alone, there were three other couples in the same situation. They worked together to find other arrangements but because they were young, there was not enough credit on their bank credit card to pay for a room, so all four couples had to share one room. Let's just say that intimacy would have to wait. Being short on cash, they found an inexpensive place to eat dinner and then went to bed. The next day as they lay in the sun, the wife began to feel something wrong with her stomach. Soon she was stuck in the restroom with a bad case of "Montezuma's Revenge". Meanwhile the husband stayed alone out in the sun where he fell asleep and became severely sunburned. Soon the stomach bug got to him as well and then they were both ill, in pain, sunburned and longing just for peace. Unfortunately, this is a true story. Paradise for them turned out to be nothing like they expected.

Before Adam and Eve ate of the fruit they were forbidden to eat, all

> **In God's presence, there can be no sickness, disease, or even worry or stress.**

was perfect. There were no weeds growing in the garden. It was heaven on earth. When I think of paradise I think of sitting by a pool next to Jesus and sipping on a cold drink. The only work involved in that is walking to the lounge chair and having to carry my towel. In the Garden the fruit was organic and juicy. I imagine green grapes the size of tennis balls, and strawberries that have to be cut and shared with others because they are too big for one person. The sun was a perfect 75 degrees Fahrenheit with lots of shade all around. What's your version of paradise?

What we do know is that Jesus was with them in the Garden. They were not separated from God in any way. Adam was with God in the garden naming God's creations and even had a part (his rib), in the creation of women.

The key to all this is that God was with them in the physical sense. His presence was with them and it did not leave them. Perfection! In God's presence, there can be no sickness, disease, or even worry or stress. Prior to the temptation at the tree of knowledge of good and evil, all thoughts were pure and holy and righteous.

Rom. 5:12 When Adam sinned, sin entered the world. Adam's sin brought death, so death spread to everyone, for everyone sinned. 13 Yes, people sinned even before the law was given. But it was not counted as sin because there was not yet any law to break.

Sin brought death into the world as we know it. We know from John 10:10 that the enemy came to steal, kill and destroy. Sickness and disease are things that destroy the body or even kill it. Sickness and disease are immature forms of death that were brought into existence through sin. Since the time Adam and Eve were removed from the garden, mankind has had to deal with all kinds of sickness and diseases. We can usually break these down into two main categories. The first is the natural things such as bacteria, viruses, physical and emotional pain, lifestyle choices and/or injuries. The second comes from the demonic realm such as curses or the spirit of infirmity. There is a third category that has kept us in bondage for the last two thousand years and that is the lie. Let me explain. When Jesus was beaten and bruised at the whipping post, crucified at the cross, and then rose from the grave, He conquered all forms of death including the immature ones we call sickness and disease. We, His children, have been redeemed from the power of sin including sickness and disease. Redeemed in this case means that we have been set free from the curse of sin and its consequences. Jesus didn't just redeem our soul so that we could go to heaven one day; He redeemed our mind, body, soul and spirit. That means that we are no longer a slave to sin, or anything that has to do with sin. But we have believed this lie that we have no power or that our power is limited to medical drugs. We have believed that Jesus died for our soul but we are still "in this world" where sickness is just a part of it. Satan is a liar. He is the father of lies, and he knows that you are redeemed. All three categories really fall under the demonic influence; sickness and disease, spirit of infirmity and the lie that we are still under their curses, are all influenced by the demonic realm. Satan has come to steal, kill and destroy and he knows his only chance is to lie. If you knew the truth, he will be crushed. The last thing the devil wants is for you to figure out the truth and believe it. He has kept the children of God in the dark for a long time and it's time he is put in his place. This is where we must look to the Bible to discover the truth and not our experiences.

Sin is not attributed when there is no law. Since Christ is the END of the Law for all who believe, sin is not imputed on us. That makes all sickness illegal no matter what its natural or spiritual roots are. The original cause was sin and that has been dealt with.

> **The last thing the devil wants is for you to figure out the truth and believe it.**

Imagine you were guilty of a crime and put in jail. The crime is sin and the jail is sickness. If the judge acquits you of the crime and you are released from jail, you would not stay one more second. You would get up and walk out and be free. That's what Jesus did for you. He paid the price and the judge, the Father, acquitted you from all penalty or punishment. We are now forgiven. And we legally have been set free from any sin. That makes any sickness illegal because sickness can only attach itself to something that has sin. To the children of God who have been redeemed, sin is an illegal attempt by the enemy to bind them up and prevent them from living as God intended and paid for. All sickness and diseases are illegal, (have no right) and are in rebellion against the finished work of the cross. That includes depression, and anxiety and the smaller forms worry and stress. You don't always need to find out why a person is sick, it is better to know how they can be set free. They may know why they are sick. What they don't know is the gospel that is the power of God unto salvation (Rom 1:16).

Sickness never originates from God. He never causes or allows any sickness for any period of time, for any reason. Yes, in the Old Testament and under the old covenant, God related to mankind according to the law. There were curses for disobedience and some of them were sickness and disease and even death. But we are no longer under the old covenant of law. God did away with those curses by making Jesus a curse for us. Therefore, all curses of the law no longer have any power. They are now illegal. Just because they are illegal does not mean that they do not exist. It is our job to let righteousness and justice be on earth as it is in Heaven. Jesus paid the price for us. It is our responsibility to enforce the redemption that Jesus died for. The enemy is a legalist, he knows that he lost, and that we are redeemed. But we know he is a liar. We must know the truth and enforce the truth anywhere he has influenced his lies. It is easy to recognize his lies. Anything that interferes with the love and truth of God is a lie. Justice is He being denied access to the children of God. Justice is the believer knowing that the price has already been paid and that they are no longer bound. Justice is the finished work of the cross providing healing and restoration for whom it was intended.

> **Anything that interferes with the love and truth of God is a lie**

If a child of God is sick in any way, it is not justice. The price has been paid for the child of God to be healthy and strong, so it is our responsibility to drive away the injustice and enforce the justice God provided for. To bring His Kingdom into our world, we must change the illegal to legal: sickness to health; death to life; curse to blessing.

We can't do that if we believe God sent the sickness, curse or death in the first place.

Matt. 12:28 ... if I am casting out demons by the Spirit of God, then the Kingdom of God has arrived among you.

My wife, Shannon, has had a lot of things to overcome in life. Most of what she has had to overcome is the lies that she believed about herself. That is not to say that she has not faced many obstacles and tragedies over her life. Things happen... then the enemy lies! When no one is there to help guide one in the truth, the enemy has a back door in to attack the truth by lying. Shannon suffered from ulcers starting at age thirteen and even a hiatal hernia by age twenty-two. She came across as energetic, loving and outgoing, but on the inside, she was a mess. Shannon was diagnosed with rheumatoid arthritis when our children were very small. At the time, we were unaware that this was illegal. We were also unaware that rheumatoid arthritis is an auto-immune disease. It is a disease where the body is attacking itself. There is a reason our bodies attack themselves. The body has a way of keeping score based on the way that we think. Shannon was tormented with the lies of the enemy. She believed that she had no value, she had believed the lies that there was no hope. They say that rheumatoid arthritis is incurable and irreversible. That kind of diagnosis is draining and removes any type of hope. Thankfully, we learned the truth. Shannon is valuable! Shannon has hope! She has been healed in every aspect of her life. Her mind is healed of the lies, her emotions are healed of depression,

> **If you say God uses sickness to teach, you might as well call the Word (Jesus), the Holy Spirit, a disease**

and fear, and her body is completely healed of rheumatoid arthritis. Chronic fatigue, Epstein bar, psoriasis, and other things that the medical field declares auto-immune and hopeless are all lies. They are immature forms of death that the enemy has planted illegally.

Did I mention that Shannon is completely healed?

Jesus spoke of a kingdom divided. He said that such a kingdom could not survive. If God heals but also makes sick, His Kingdom is divided. Therefore, He doesn't cause sickness.

If God gives life but also kills, His Kingdom is divided. Therefore, He doesn't kill. If God blesses but also curses, His Kingdom is divided. Therefore, He doesn't curse. God never uses sickness to teach us a lesson. He has the Word (2 Tim 3:16), The Holy Spirit (John 16:13) and the Anointing (1 John 2:27) to do that. If you say God uses sickness to teach, you might as well call the Word (Jesus), the Holy Spirit, a disease. If God were to use sickness as a lesson, then we should pray for the symptoms to worsen so we can really learn our lesson. If one believes God teaches through sickness, then one is in conscious willful rebellion against His will if one goes to the doctor to seek help. If sickness were from God to draw us to Him, we should pray that every member of our family becomes sick with cancer so we all can draw near to God. You wouldn't wish that on anyone, why do think God would? If sickness were from God, then going to God for healing would mean that we are going to the very being that is causing our destruction to be set free from our

> **If you say God uses sickness to teach, you might as well call the Word (Jesus), the Holy Spirit, a disease**

destruction. That's like going to ask the school bully for protection from himself.

So how do we treat sickness? It doesn't matter which form of sickness is showing up, treat it the same. Christianity 101: If it's a sickness, heal it. If it's a demon, cast it out. If it's a curse, break it. If it's a lie, exchange it with the truth. Treat all sickness the same whether it is caused naturally or physically. Destruction is the work of the devil. All it takes for devil to have his way is for a few believers to do nothing. Even doctors know sickness is bad and that is why they devoted their entire lives to eradicating it. Medicine is not divine, it is merely a natural way of producing healing but it has its flaws. (Cost, side effects, misdiagnosis, fallibility) We are not against doctors or medicine; we are simply for God and His Kingdom. This is about divine healing, not natural remedies or diets. This is about our identity in Christ and the enforcing of what He provided. Jesus has given you power and authority, but we must learn to enforce it.

We cannot enforce what we do not have the power to enforce. John 8:32 says that the truth will set us free. "The truth", the Word of God is filled with all the power and authority we need. But we must know the Truth. The truth cannot set us free unless we know it and enforce it in our lives. The lie must be combatted. The lie must be exposed. As long as it is not exposed, it is believed to be truth and therefore influences our lives. To enforce the truth in our lives we must grow in our knowledge of the truth.

The devil comes to steal, kill and destroy. He is the origin of lies. The Bible says that he goes around roaring like a lion. Notice it did not say he looks like a lion or has power like a lion. He is not powerful. He is quite powerless. He has already been defeated and all power and authority have been taken from Him. Jesus took back all authority at the resurrection. Jesus said, "all authority has been given to me", that means that the devil has none. He simply has the lie. His only game is deception. As long as we, the children of God, embrace his lies we will be forever shackled and chained. The devil is the father of lies, even his roar is a lie.

Section 4

Overcoming Lies and Killing Depression

6   God Will Work With You

Rom. 15:18-19 *Yet I dare not boast about anything except what Christ has done through me, bringing the Gentiles to God by my message and by the way I worked among them.* *19 They were convinced by the power of miraculous signs and wonders and by the power of God's Spirit. In this way, I have fully presented the Good News of Christ from Jerusalem all the way to Illyricum.*

Once I had the blessing of taking elementary kids to camp. It was amazing to see so many little ones worshipping and praising God all in one place. God was moving powerfully among the students, it was evident that He was there, loving them, healing hearts and setting them free. There was a young lady in a wheel chair that had broken her foot the first day of camp. When she returned from the hospital I had the opportunity to pray for her healing, but to my dismay, NOTHING! The second night of camp we prayed again. And again, NOTHING. The third night of camp we were determined to see the pain leave and for her to walk and dance again, but NOTHING. The Lord said that we need the faith of children, I felt if there was ever enough faith for a healing this was it, but we were unsuccessful so far. On the last night of camp, we gave it another shot, we prayed but she was still in pain, so we prayed again. I heard this little voice from a tiny person praying. It captured my attention like a gun going off in a silent room. I became fixated for a moment on this voice. I told this little one to lay hands on the broken foot and command it to be healed. She prayed one time for about ten seconds. The foot was healed! The injured girl's mom was a nurse so she took off the temporary cast and the girl walked, then jumped, and then danced and praised the Lord. I must admit that when I was alone, I complained to God like Jonah did after Nineveh repented. I was upset that I prayed multiple times, but it was a little eight-year-old that prayed once, and the foot was healed.

When we are walking in our identity as a son of the living God, we become powerful agents of His Kingdom building process.

Mark 16:20 And the disciples went everywhere and preached, and the Lord worked through them, confirming what they said by many miraculous signs.

Did the disciples just go and imitate Jesus? Did they hear what the Father was doing and join in? Did they hear what the Father was saying and repeat it? Or did they just go out and spread the gospel and God just happened to do some (many) miraculous signs. Then we must ask, was this just for the twelve disciples and then Paul after his conversion or does this extend to others including you and me?

There are a couple of schools of thought concerning the title of this chapter. Some believe and follow the idea that God is sovereign and we are just to watch what He does and live with it. They say if it were God's will to be different, it would be different. We know that Jesus said, He only does what He sees the Father doing and He only speaks what He hears the Father saying. Some say God changes his mind; or, even that he will do what we His children have spoken or declared, even if it was not part of His plan. There have been many arguments between theologians regarding this mystery and I do not wish to start one here! But we must look at a few examples in the scriptures to see what God's heart is and what His plans are, to at least answer the question, does God work with us to confirm His Word?

For the sake of avoiding an argument let's say we agree that God knows what He is doing. That He has a plan, and that He partners with humanity to carry out his plan. After all He is the King of His Kingdom. The Kingdom of God is the reign, dominion and supremacy of God over everything.

Matt. 12:28 *But if I am casting out demons by the Spirit of God, then the Kingdom of God has arrived among you.*

Let's begin with the topic the disciples were preaching about. Were they declaring the death, burial, and resurrection of Jesus? No, that was coming in the near future, and they didn't even understand it when Jesus told them (Luke 9:44, 45). They went out and preached the Kingdom of God was at hand. As they were preaching that the Kingdom of God is at hand, they demonstrated it with signs, wonders and miracles, healing the sick and casting out demons. The Kingdom of God being here now is the good news that the Jews had been waiting for. But the Jews were looking for a different version of the kingdom. When we share something that is different to what people expect, it is not always welcomed. But the miracles are hard to ignore. The Kingdom of God is not just a teaching for all to follow. It is the power of God going forward to take back from the enemy what Adam lost. I mean that it is not just words to convince someone in an argument. It is backed with power from God.

1 Thess. 1:5 For when we brought you the Good News, it was not only with words but also with power, for the Holy Spirit gave you full assurance that what we said was true. And you know of our concern for you from the way we lived when we were with you.

The gospel without the power is missing the fullness of the blessing. Paul makes it clear that unless the power of God is behind the Word of God, it is not complete.

Rom. 15:18-19 ... I dare not boast about anything except what Christ has done through me, bringing the Gentiles to God by my message and by the way I worked among them. 19 They were convinced by the power of miraculous signs and wonders and by the power of God's Spirit. In this way, I have fully presented the Good News of Christ from Jerusalem all the way to Illyricum.

He again makes it known that he was not a very good preacher but that he was backed by the power of God.

1 Cor. 2:4-5 And my message and my preaching were very plain. Rather than using clever and persuasive speeches, I relied only on the power of the Holy Spirit. 5 I did this so you would trust not in human wisdom but in the power of God.

The Kingdom of God is evidenced by displays of power and authority. As Children of God we have everything that we need. We are His children and we are full of the Holy Spirit; the same Holy Spirit that rested on Jesus, the same Holy Spirit that empowered Paul and the disciples. The Kingdom of God is not in the talking about it, it is in the demonstrating of it.

*1 Cor. 4:20 For the Kingdom of God is not just a lot of talk; **it is living by God's power.***

The Kingdom of God breaks through in a display of God's power because it is a Kingdom of power. He reigns supreme and He is all-powerful. It started with Jesus demonstrating the Kingdom. He eradicated sickness and disease and He cast out demons. He raised the dead!

Acts 10:38 . . . And you know that God anointed Jesus of Nazareth with the Holy Spirit and with power. Then Jesus went around doing good and healing all who were oppressed by the devil, for God was with him.

We are His children and we are full of the Holy Spirit; the same Holy Spirit that rested on Jesus, the same Holy Spirit that empowered Paul and the disciples.

One of the main reasons that people followed Jesus is because of the miracles He performed. Let's face it, human nature drives us to see the supernatural. We go see shows about magicians and wonder how they do what they do. We are always looking for the "trick", the sleight of hand, the deception. Jesus was doing things no one else could do. The blind would receive their sight, the deaf could hear, even the dead were raised back to life. When it comes to sharing the Gospel, God does not mess around. He backs it with power. He proves that there is no trick, no deceit. His words are backed with miraculous power. Jesus even said that if there is no demonstration of power, then don't believe me.

John 10:37-38 Don't believe me unless I carry out my Father's work. *38 But if I do his work, believe in the evidence of the miraculous works I have done, even if you don't believe me. Then you will know and understand that the Father is in me, and I am in the Father."*

"Believe in the evidence", Jesus said. As I mentioned before, we are always looking for the trick behind the act. I can understand how the Pharisees would be at least a little suspicious, or even not believe. But they investigated the miracles and found them to be true. In their hardness of heart they ignored the signs and made excuses. And when the Pharisees asked Him when the Kingdom would come he replied,

Luke 17: 20"The Kingdom of God can't be detected by visible signs. 21 You won't be able to say, 'Here it is!' or 'It's over there!' For the Kingdom of God is already among you.

Wait a minute! The Kingdom of God can't be among us already for we are still here on earth. I was always taught that one day I'll get to heaven, but until then I am stuck here in the world. This took me a long time to process and figure out. My mind could not wrap around the words of Jesus without confusion because I was thinking in natural terms. We must learn to let go of our natural thoughts, those from the carnal mind and learn to replace

> **We bring the Kingdom to earth by casting out demons, healing the sick, and sharing the gospel to all corners of the earth.**

them with the supernatural thoughts from the mind of the Spirit. We serve a God who is supernatural. If He is supernatural then the supernatural is natural to him. We can be on the earth (the kingdom of the enemy) and live according to the supernatural Kingdom of God. We have grown up learning that there are just some things you can't mess with. They are law! Things such as Gravity. Seriously, don't mess with gravity, you will lose. Even things like the weather.

We don't have any say over the weather. But wait a minute. Let's look back into history where we see Jesus walking on water, Elijah praying for rain, Jesus calming the storm. You may say, well that was Jesus and Elijah was a prophet. But remember that Jesus said we were going to do the same works, even greater works.

John 14:12 "*I tell you the truth, anyone who believes in me will do the same works I have done, and even greater works, because I am going to be with the Father.*"

Let me remind you of the story I told earlier of my calming the wind for my own benefit. Here we have a great example of living in the natural world but bringing the supernatural into it. In other words, bringing the Kingdom of God into the kingdom of the earth. What or where is the Kingdom you ask? Kingdom of God is in every believer, in every follower of Christ and it is to be released by the believer into the natural world. We bring the Kingdom to earth by casting out demons, healing the sick, and sharing the gospel to all corners of the earth.

As we renew or minds to the likeness of Christ, we are transformed from the natural to the supernatural. We have been given the mind of Christ, we just have to learn to turn it on and shut the old one off. That's the simple explanation of the transformed mind. Having a transformed mind enables us to release the Kingdom into the lives of those who need it, when they need it, in any and all situations.

Mark 16:15-18 And then he told them, "Go into all the world and preach the Good News to everyone.¹⁶ Anyone who believes and is baptized will be saved. But anyone who refuses to believe will be condemned. ¹⁷ These miraculous signs will accompany those who believe: They will cast out demons in my name, and they will speak in new languages. ¹⁸ They will be able to handle snakes with safety, and if they drink anything poisonous, it won't hurt them. They will be able to place their hands on the sick, and they will be healed."

To preach or to release the Kingdom of God is to proclaim God's reign and rule over everything. The devil is no longer in charge, he has been defeated. When Jesus was crucified, descended into the depths and took the keys of authority back, and then was raised from the dead, He regained all authority. That means the devil has none. Even though we walk on the earth, the Kingdom of God has come and is among us now. Let me suggest that it is our responsibility to continue to grow in the knowledge and power of what that means.

We will forever be learning what grace has done for us. The real question remains, how much power and authority do we have to release the Kingdom and to what degree?

The question to be answered is, will God work through you? Do we need to hear God's voice before we act? Do we need to see God move before we move? God has already moved (the Cross), and God has already spoken, "GO". Our role is just to step out in faith and see what God will do. Go pray for the sick, give sight to the blind eyes, open the deaf ears, and cast out the demons. Release the oppressed and the depressed, the stressed, and the worriers.

If you want to see the Kingdom of God come through you, there is only one way. Step out in faith and start praying and believing. Pray for the sick and believe that they will be healed. Believe because you commanded with the authority that has been given to you by Jesus. Believe because we know that Jesus wants to heal. There is no formula, so look to Jesus as the example and follow His lead. He told the demon to leave, he didn't ask the Father to remove it. He took authority over the sickness or the disease and removed it Himself. Remember Jesus gave you all authority, that means that the demon you are casting out has none, and must obey. We are bringing the rule and reign of God to the earth. We are not fighting the demonic, we are ruling them. As a follower of Christ, you are filled with the Holy Spirit and have all authority. That is really great news but it may be hard to let sink in. It makes perfect sense when we hear it, but putting it into practice and believing it as fact can be difficult.

> **We are not fighting the demonic, we are ruling them**

Keep pressing in and pressing on. After a service one night we were praying for the sick and a young man walked up and told me he was having surgery the next day to remove a cyst from his side. He lifted his shirt and there it was on his right side at the base of the rib cage. As I put my hand on the cyst it was the size of tennis ball cut in half. It was definitely big enough for me to feel in the palm of my hand. I started to pray, but only a few words came out, "In Jesus Name". I was planning on a more lengthy prayer, but as I said "Jesus" it disappeared. I stopped, somewhat shocked that it was gone so quickly, and asked him if I was crazy, or was it gone already. He confirmed that it was completely gone. Another time I was on a ministry trip with some students and I came across a woman that had a sling on her arm. It was the kind that strapped her arm to her side to make her shoulder immobile. We had just arrived at the church, there had not been any worship or teaching yet, but God doesn't care. I asked her if I could pray for her shoulder and she graciously and hopefully said, "yes". She had torn her rotator cuff just two weeks earlier and was in a lot of pain. The pastor of the church, her husband and some from my team said a quick prayer commanding healing, just like Jesus would have done. I asked her if there was any way she could test it without damaging or aggravating the injury. Her husband helped her remove the first strap giving her a little mobility, then another strap, then the sling came off. As you can guess the shoulder ended up with full mobility and no pain. Five days later I received a text from the pastor and it said that she had gone back to her doctor and received a clean bill of health. It was miraculously healed. Anyone who has had a shoulder injury knows that they take a year or more for full mobility and usage to return.

1 Cor. 10:13. . . Whatever you eat or drink, or whatever you do, do it all for the glory of God.

God has given us a directive to "go!" He did not make it clear on how but He did give us the why. Go and build the Kingdom of God. He wants to partner with you and use your skills and abilities and your creativity. You don't have to wait for a specific direction with an exact order. If it is in your heart to do something for God, then do it! That is what He will get behind. He will get behind your dreams and your visions and He will work in direct correlation with your faith. This means He will work with you in ministry and in life outside of ministry. He will work with you in business, arts, science, media and anything else you can think of. God will work with you, just remember to ask the Holy Spirit to be involved and then trust your heart.

7 Performance Mentality

2 Tim. 2:15

Work hard so you can present yourself to God and

receive his approval. Be a good worker, one who does

not need to be ashamed and who correctly explains the

word of truth

As a child growing up I played on a lot of sports teams. It would be an understatement to call me competitive. I have an older brother who also played sports, and most of my friends and I wanted to be the best. It was not good enough for me to be on the team. It was not good enough for me to be on the field as opposed to the bench. I wanted to be the best, the star, the "alpha dog" that hits the winning hit, or scores the winning goal. And "losing sucks," was another understatement. Anyone who plays sports knows that the best players play, and the others get to play when your team is way ahead or way behind. Those who can perform and help the team get a win will be those on the field as much as possible. We watch this in professional sports all the time. There are players on the sidelines who rarely get in and then there are those who rarely come out. Those on the sideline are just waiting for their chance, but hoping that it doesn't come at the cost of the starter getting injured, NOBODY HOPES FOR THAT!!!! If you believe that, you were never a second-string player. Even when the injured starter comes back from injury, he or she always gets the job back.

The same goes for our schooling growing up. When we perform and the grade on the little piece of paper is closer to the beginning of the alphabet, mom and dad are happy and proud. When we don't

> **Your relationship with God has nothing to do with your performance**

perform the grade slips away from the top, mom and dad are not happy and they let you know how disappointed they are. I'll be fair and say that some moms and dads are less emotional about their kid's grades, but most are fairly demanding and responsive to the outcome. Performance is the way the world operates. Jobs are on the line, getting accepted into college, salaries, getting the right spouse maybe, or in some cases keeping a spouse, are all based on performance. Competing against the next guy is and will always be the way the world operates. There is always someone better nipping at your heals for your spot.

Then we go to church and we are taught what to do and what not to do. The Bible has plenty of rules or laws that we are to follow. And we have been led to believe that if we want to be on God's good side, we better do them well or follow them correctly. Your relationship with God has nothing to do with your performance! Your

relationship with God has nothing to do with your performance!

Your relationship with God has nothing to do with your

performance! Your relationship with God has nothing to do with

your performance!

2 Tim. 2:15 Work hard so you can present yourself to God and receive

his approval. Be a good worker, one who does not need to be ashamed

and who correctly explains the word of truth. Doesn't that sound just

like your parent or your teacher or whoever it is you are trying to

impress? Now what I'm about to say, read with caution, many will

shutter in fear and call it blasphemy. I assure you it is not and as we

look at the Bible you will see I am right. The whole Bible was written

for you, but the whole Bible was not written to you. That's why Paul

tells us to work hard to understand it so that we can learn who God

is and what He really wants from us. There is an Old Testament, a

collection of books, written to show the old covenant that God made

with Moses and the Israelites. It was written to show that MAN

COULD NOT PERFORM WELL ENOUGH to please God. Man could not

even come close. It was also written to point to the future covenant

and to the Messiah who would usher it in. Covenant governs how

God relates to His people. The covenant that you are under, determines how God relates to you. We must learn how to relate to God through the covenant that He sets. Let me say this really clearly, and then I will explain in detail. Your relationship with God has nothing to do with your performance! It is called GRACE. It is free, and it provides freedom from law and rules, and it is bathed in LOVE, the love of the Father.

John 1:17 For the law was given through Moses, but God's unfailing love and faithfulness came through Jesus Christ.

Everything you are is because of Jesus and what He did. Everything you try to do is as filthy rags, the Bible says. (Isa. 64:6) The term "filthy rags" is used to describe a dirty bandage that was covering an infectious wound. Your righteousness on your own apart from Christ, is as gross as that infected bandage.

The new covenant is far superior to the old. In 2 Cor. 3, Paul describes the old covenant when Moses came down of the mountain holding the Ten Commandments and his face was glowing with the Glory of God even through a veil. It also says that the Glory was fading already. It ends in death. The writer says how much more should we expect of the Glory of God under the new covenant now that the Holy Spirit is giving life. The new covenant makes it clear that we are "right with God." The old required our performance, which we could not do well at all. The new is based on the finished work of Jesus, and it is finished. We are made right with God. No more performing, no more trying, no more feeling like failures every time we miss the mark.

Rom. 8:1 *So now there is no condemnation for those who belong to Christ Jesus.*

There is NO MORE condemnation. You are right with God and it will not be taken away from you.

I grew up in church and they told me about grace and told me that I was saved by grace, but they still required the law. The teachers had great hearts and meant well, but they had not rightly divided the scriptures and were still teaching us to focus on the law instead of the grace of God. Jesus tells a parable in Matt. 9 about putting new wine into old wine skins or patching old clothes with a new piece of cloth. It doesn't work. You can't learn about the grace that Jesus provides when you are being taught the Law. My mentors had me so focused on not sinning, that not sinning was all I could think about. Jesus was trying to tell us to throw out the old, and stop focusing on the law.

We cannot get to the core of our identity until we understand that the performance mentality, as much as it is required to succeed in the world's eyes, must be eliminated from our thinking in regards to our relationship with God. If we don't get this concept, then we always will be trying to do God's job. Then when things go wrong we will put the blame on him. Our faith will always be on a rollercoaster of disbelief and self-condemnation. We will still be focusing on the problem not the solution, and we will judge others for not performing to our level or standard. Our faith will always be works based and we will confuse people by ministering condemnation and guilt. Let me explain!

I was taught as a child and even as a young adult in church that I needed to get rid of sin in my life. Stop sinning! Well that led me to focus on sin, (the problem) instead of on Jesus, (the solution). I compared myself to other Christians or even worse to those who didn't know the truth about the Gospel. I condemned them or myself in the comparison. I was problem focused. When I had been to camp, or a retreat, I was high, but when I had been struggling in my sin, I was low. I didn't even know how confused I was at the time. I so badly wanted to walk in the Spirit, but I was stuck walking in the flesh because in my mind I had to get rid of my bad self. For thousands of years man tried to get right with God on his own by following the law. It doesn't work. You can't change your old nature, it has to be killed! It must be crucified with Christ. The problem is I was focused on trying to change my old self. No one can get rid of his or her own sin. It is impossible; it's what the old covenant which leads to death called for and proved we were not capable of. When I came to an understanding of who I was in Christ, and who He was in me, I no longer had to focus on Sin. His blood already paid the price. I am no longer just a sinner saved by grace, I am a saint (Rom. 1:7, 1 Cor. 1:2), I am the righteousness of Christ (Phil. 1:11), I am holy (Col 3:12, 1 Pet 1:15), I am pure (1 John 3:3) and so much more. It wasn't because of me, it was because of

> His blood already paid the price. I am no longer a sinner saved by grace, I am a saint

Jesus. He made me that way. He wasn't making me that way; He made me that way. Already done, finished, the game is over. Now I can simply focus on His love, His mercy and His grace, which causes me to keep my eyes on Him, and as my eyes are on Him I am not drawn to the things of the flesh. As I look to Jesus, He is transforming me more and more into His image taking me from Glory to Glory. (2 Cor. 3:18)

Now "good works" comes natural, not as a performance but as an evidence of His love for me, and my love for Him. I do not lack confidence to do His work for I know who I am. I now have confidence because I am a child of God filled with the Holy Spirit, anointed to share His love with the world. My identity is in Christ alone. If I fail, I am still His and in right standing with Him. Of course, this is not a license to sin. It is a position from which I stand. When I stand as a righteous, pure, and holy man of God, I am focused on God's presence in my life, and it is in His presence that sin has no power over me.

Jesus said that He no longer calls us slaves, but now he calls us friends. That means that at one time we were slaves. Slaves work hard to do the work that is given them but they are not given any benefits. Slaves are not in on the meetings where plans and policies are made. Slaves are not told why they are working and they have no say in when to start or stop for the day. There is no relationship between the master and the slave. When we first hear the gospel and receive it into our hearts and become saved, it is almost like we become His slave. We are told what to do to act like Christ but we really

> **When you are a friend of God, you get to sit with Him and make plans with Him, maybe even sway him from one plan to another.**

don't know the Father very well. We may not know Him well, but He calls us His friends. We know He loves us and that's enough to go to work.

As we grow in our relationship with the Father, we get pruned like a farmer prunes a vine. When a grape vine is full grown, then the fruit grows on the vine. The vine, however, keeps growing, but it does not grow any fruit on it. A lot of energy is spent on the growth of that vine that is not producing fruit, so it is cut off just at the place where the fruit ends. This is what the Father does to us. Yes, this can be painful, but it is really glorious when you think about it. If we are at the point where our work becomes meaningless, then we should be stopped. Working for no reason is the worst kind of work. When He prunes us, all of our energy is spent on the fruit of our lives. We mature, and there is where we are called His friends. God tells a slave what to do, but God tells a friend what He is thinking. Friends know what to do and why.   There is a purpose and a joy that comes from the work being done. A friend gets to be a part of the meeting where plans are being made. A friend gets to find out the plan before he sets out to complete the task. And most importantly, a friend has a say in the matter as well. When you are a friend of God, you get to sit with Him and make plans with Him, maybe even sway him from one plan to another.

We see evidence of this in a couple of examples. First, we see Abraham negotiating with God in the story of Sodom and Gomorrah in Gen. 18. God came to Abraham and said He was going destroy the cities and all the people including women and children. From a law perspective, they deserved what God had planned. They were vile to say the least. But Abraham was able to calm God down, and get Him to rethink His plan. Lot, a relative of Abraham, and his family were saved from the destruction.

Then we see a similar event with Moses and the Israelites. The Israelites were the chosen ones whom God had rescued from hundreds of years of slavery. God not only delivered them from their captors, He demolished them and had the entire army drowned as they tried to follow the Israelites across the bottom of the Red Sea. The Israelites had a slave mentality. After over four hundred years, it was all they knew. They were used to being told what to do just to survive. Now they are in the wilderness, and God is hanging out with them as a friend. He is leading them to the Promise Land and preparing them to take ownership of their own land and be free. I think it is fair to say that the Israelites were stubborn, whiney, complainers that didn't know how to be friends with the master. After many miracles, signs, and wonders, God was tired of the complaints and the disobedience. He told His friend Moses that He was going to destroy the people. Moses, like Abraham began to negotiate with God (Nunbers 14:13).

I find it fascinating that Moses and Abraham had the audacity to argue with the Creator of all things. To argue or negotiate with God was not a form of disrespect and it was not a lack of honor. Moses

> **When we grow in our understanding of God's heart, and become a friend of God, we learn that we no longer have to perform to please Him**

and Abraham each had experiences with God where they learned where they stood with the Master. They understood what it meant to be in God's presence, be in awe of His Glory and comfortably at ease at the same time. Moses even told the Lord that unless God went with them, that he did not want to go (Ex 33:15).

When we grow in our understanding of God's heart, and become a friend of God, we learn that we no longer have to perform to please Him. The most amazing part of this, is that Moses was under the old covenant and had not received the Holy Spirit. And somehow Moses understood the value of God's presence. The Holy Spirit is the presence of God in our lives each and every moment. He is our comforter, our guide, our strength, our peace, He will never leave you nor forsake you, and He is our friend. There is a perfect tension between God being our God and our friend. As God, we honor Him, revere Him and fear Him, and in that we would never talk back to Him. As friend, we can boldly approach His throne and bring our request to Him.

If we read the Bible from a legalistic perspective, we might see all the rules or laws and feel an obligation to work hard to follow them. The main problem with this perspective is that we would become problem focused, making us feel the need to perform. But, when we read the Word of God as a love letter of grace, we fall in love with the author and perfecter of our faith (Heb. 12:2). It is easier and much more enjoyable to be in love with the one who has already paid the price for the things that we feel obligated to perform. It is Love focused! It is peace focused! It is freedom focused! And in His presence, temptation ceases.

8   Grace Yourself

"How unhappy is he who cannot forgive himself."

Publilius Syrus

The other day I was walking through a store with my friend Kyle

Dickerson, as we shopped with my wife and daughter. As we got

close to the cash register I noticed that the young man working was

dressed like a girl, wearing full make up and talking very feminine. I had to take a double take as you could imagine, because this is not something I see very often.

Here is the divide in the road. Our natural mind and heart see this young man as less than he really is. Even though we have been taught to treat others the way we want to be treated, we may just avoid all conversation with a person such as this one. We don't want to judge or condemn so we just avoid, but really the judgment has already happened. God gives us a grace that allows us to see a young man like this and realize his full potential. He was created in the image of God and God's thoughts of him are good. God has a plan for this young man, maybe he does not know it yet, but God still cares for and loves him and has given us the ability to love him unconditionally as He does. Kyle said to me, "I just want to go up and give that young man a big loving hug, and tell him how valuable he is, and that Jesus loves him". That is the mind of Christ. That is a man who is allowing the grace of God to flow through him towards others.

2 Peter 1:3 God has given us everything we need for living a Godly life.

That is Grace! God has graced us and empowered us to live a life of Godliness. So what does God mean when He says we can live a Godly life? Godly means God-like, it means living a life where sin has no hold on you, sin has no power over you. Think for a moment how hard it is to live a sin free life. No one has ever done that except Jesus. The book of 1 John makes it clear that we cannot claim to be without sin. But what if this Grace that God gives is so powerful it assists us in overcoming the stronghold that sin has on our life.

> **Grace is ours, we just need to open our eyes with the help of the Holy Spirit to see just how powerful this Grace really is.**

What if the Grace that God offers is so powerful that we no longer struggle with things that used to ensnare or trap us in sin. Let me take this a little bit further. What if the Grace of God is powerful enough to help us overcome, walk away from temptation as if we are not really even tempted.

What if there is no fear of man, no fear of failure, no fear of inadequacy, no fear of lack; it is a life of complete peace, faith, hope and love. This is obviously not something we can do on our own. We could never accomplish that in a million years. It is a supernatural act of God called Grace. Every believer has been given this gift to the fullest extent. It is the second greatest treasure that God has given to us on this earth after salvation itself. But it is hidden, hidden from our minds, our thoughts and our faith because the enemy simply has blinded us. He is a liar and a thief. His only game is to try and steal, kill and destroy us by blinding us from the power that God has already given us. Grace is ours, we just need to open our eyes with the help of the Holy Spirit to see just how powerful this Grace really is.

We believe what we believe based on our past experiences, our upbringing, and what we have learned in church or from the world. Most people have heard of the golden rule, "do unto others as you would have them do to you." The Bible calls it reaping what you sow, but it is a universal truth all around the world. I can still hear my grandmother saying to treat others the way you want to be treated. This is a belief that most of the world teaches in some way or another. It's a very simple concept of humanity that has its author in the Creator of all things.

The Bible makes it very clear that we are to love one another. Loving one another is different from simply treating others the way you want to be treated. I can look at someone with disgust, and still treat him or her with kindness. My actions may be Godly but my thoughts are not even close. To truly love we must learn to see others from God's perspective. To see them with the same love that He sees them, to be willing to lay down your life for them if needed. It is impossible to judge someone to be less than who they are in God's eyes, and love them at the same time.

> It is impossible to judge someone to be less than who they are in God's eyes, and love them at the same time.

That's where the difficulty comes. It's hard not to judge. Even though the Bible tells us not to judge, we cannot do that without understanding Grace and the power that is has. People can be mean! People can be vulgar! People can be sinful! This is how we naturally see people. When we see them through our own perspective it is easy to judge because we see them in comparison to ourselves by what we have been taught or experienced. When we compare

> **But you can't give grace to others unless you Grace yourself first.**

someone to ourselves, we are using a scale that God has already done away with. When Christ died, the law was done away with. Grace is the new scale. We must learn to see others from God's perspective, through His supernatural eyes.

When we understand that our righteousness is from God and that we cannot be righteous apart from Him, then we begin to understand grace. We cannot be right with God apart from Him making us right with Him. So out of His grace He made us right with Him, and then He gave more grace just to help us understand what He had done. I can't even claim to understand grace without His grace. We have been given a very powerful tool by God to live a Godly life. It's called Grace! But you can't give grace to others, unless you grace yourself first. You can't love others, unless you love yourself first. You can't give peace to others, unless you have peace yourself. Jesus taught us this principle when He slept through a deadly storm in the front of a boat. Because His peace was greater than the storm, He could release peace over the storm and it ceased

Luke 8: They came to Jesus and woke Him up, saying, "Master, Master, we are perishing!" And He got up and rebuked the wind and the surging waves, and they stopped, and it became calm.

We cannot release to others what we do not have for ourselves. How can I treat others with love if I cannot treat myself with love? How can I forgive others if I don't know how to forgive myself? Let me explain.

As hard as it is to not judge others, it is even harder not to judge ourselves. We are harder on ourselves than anyone else. We punish ourselves for not being perfect. Everyone knows that no one is perfect, but we judge ourselves as if we are supposed to be. We are our own worst critic! Why? The Bible says that the devil is the accuser of the brethren. The devil does his best to stand between you and God and accuse you of every wrongdoing, he is not looking at God when he does this, he is looking at you. His goal is to take your mind and thoughts off the power of Grace, off forgiveness, and to make you think you are less than you really are. Because we don't know how to grace ourselves (this includes forgiving ourselves,) we believe his accusations and punish ourselves. The key word there is "believe." Do you **believe** that God has forgiven you? Do you **believe** that God has made you right with Him and that it has nothing to do with your own merits? Do you **believe** that God has separated you from your sins, as far as the East is from the West? We say we believe, until the enemy stands in between God and us and accuses us, then we are not sure. His accusations are lies. He may be pointing out a truth, a sin that you committed. But that sin was paid for and is not part of you anymore. It is part of the old you, not the new creation that God made you. The devil is a legalist and will do his best to get you to be a legalist with him. He will remind you of the illegal (sinful) acts that you have committed. If you believe him, you will feel guilty and shameful. You will feel the effects of sin that have already been paid for. Every sin, past present and future has already been paid for by Christ on the cross. That's why the devil stands between God and us; he wants us to forget that our sins have been covered by the Blood of Jesus. He wants to block your view of the truth. There is a big difference between facts and the truth. Fact: you have missed the mark of God, and it is called sin. Truth: God has redeemed you and paid for your sin and you are no longer bound by that sin. There is an old hymn that says, "Turn your eyes upon Jesus, look full in His wonderful face. And the things of earth will grow strangely dim, in the light of His glory and grace." When we are being accused, feeling lonely, worried, depressed, or even stressed, the best thing to do is follow the advice in that song. Turn your eyes on Jesus and away from yourself. The devil is accusing you and getting you to look at yourself apart from the work of the cross. Stop! And look to the finished work of the cross, and how you benefit from it. When Christ went to the cross, for the joy set before Him, He had already seen every sin you would ever commit. There is nothing that will shock Him or even disappoint Him anymore. He no longer sees your sin. For Him to see your sin, He would have to deny the very work that He already accomplished. If we are going to have the mind of Christ and learn to think like He does, we will have to learn to grace ourselves and ignore the accusations of the enemy.

I can't imagine what it must have been like for Peter on the night before the crucifixion. We all know that Peter denied Christ three times. Peter was one of the first disciples and one of the three closest to Jesus. Jesus was his best friend. The first denial was a simple defense from the late-night crowd that was watching as Jesus was being arrested. He was just trying to stay close and keep watch on his best friend; he didn't want to be slowed down, he didn't have time for questioning. The second denial was a little more direct because, the tension was growing, the crowds were getting larger and the accusation was being confirmed by more than one. The last denial was a direct, "I don't know Him"! An emphatic statement, that Peter himself, was innocent of their accusation, but the statement itself was anything but innocent. He was guilty and he knew it. More than that, He was guilty of denying his best friend. A friend is one who stands by your side no matter what, and Peter had gone the way of the crowd, he had become a

> **If we are going to have the mind of Christ and learn to think like He does, we will have to learn to grace ourselves and ignore the accusations of the enemy.**

traitor. If anyone had the right to feel guilty and shameful it was Peter. I'm sure he was devastated and heartbroken to say the least. I can just imagine the enemy pointing his finger at Peter and making every accusation in the book to destroy Peter's faith. The devil wanted to take Peter out of the game.

The reason I bring up this story is to show you how Jesus responded. The story of Peter's denial is a tragic one and we can all relate it in some degree or another. The bigger the tragedy of sin, the bigger the Grace of our amazing Father in heaven. The amazing story of the Father's heart is in John 21. Jesus has risen from the tomb and has appeared to the disciples for a third time. Peter and some of the others had gone back to doing what they did before Jesus called them; they were fishing. We tend to go back to doing what we know, when we are heartbroken and full of guilt and shame. Jesus calls out to them from the shore and invites them to come in and have some breakfast.

John 21:15-19 After breakfast Jesus asked Simon Peter, "Simon son of John, do you love me more than these?" "Yes, Lord," Peter replied, "you know I love you." "Then feed my lambs," Jesus told him. 16 Jesus repeated the question: "Simon son of John, do you love me?" "Yes, Lord," Peter said, "you know I love you." "Then take care of my sheep," Jesus said. [17] A third time he asked him, "Simon son of John, do you love me?" Peter was hurt that Jesus asked the question a third time. He said, "Lord, you know everything. You know that I love you." Jesus said, "Then feed my sheep. [18] "I tell you the truth, when you were young, you were able to do as you liked; you dressed yourself and went wherever you wanted to go. But when you are old, you will stretch out your hands, and others will dress you and take you where you don't want to go." [19] Jesus said this to let him know by what kind of death he would glorify God. Then Jesus told him, "Follow me."

Jesus asked Peter three times if he loved Him. One time for every time he had denied Him. We must understand that God had already forgiven Peter. Peter did not need to make up for the times he had denied Jesus. This was not a re-do for God's sake, this was a re-do for Peter's sake. Peter needed to know that he was not only forgiven, but still loved and adored and anointed to carry the Gospel. Peter did not realize during the questioning what was going on. The shame he had caused him to be a little defensive. Peter said, "Lord you know everything and you know that I love you," but what he really was saying was, "lay off, I feel guilty enough already." The Father was doing what only He can do, taking what had already been restored by the resurrection and showing it to the one He had restored.

The Father has not only restored all things but out of His great love for us, he wants us to know that we are restored as well, that we are right with Him. We must simply understand how powerful His grace is and what it means for us. He has given us the power to live a godly life. A life free from worry! A life free from guilt! A life free from shame! A life free from sin! That's the power of grace! Grace yourself!

9 Dream Big

"Dream lofty dreams, and as you dream, so shall you become. Your vision is the promise of what you shall one day be; your ideal is the prophecy of what you shall at last unveil." – *James Allen*

Children are amazing to watch when they are just free and in their element. Watching a young boy play with his firetruck and imagining himself driving it. He will make all the sounds of the truck with his mouth, raise the ladder, climb up it with his little fireman figurine and put out the blazing inferno. That child is dreaming and he doesn't even know it. He has no inhibitions or fears of what life may become because he has not learned any yet. He hasn't learned that he might be incapable or inadequate. He has not been told that something is impossible. He is without knowing it, seeing life with great vision and dreaming of a life that is awesome and full of excitement.

What is it that you want in life? Have you ever stopped to just dream of what life should be like for you? All of us have dreams, but not all of us know how to dream right. Not all of us know how to dream the way God intended. Not many know how to dream with God. Prov. 29:18 tells us that we need to have a vision of the future or we will perish. What are we looking forward to? What do we hope to accomplish? Those are great questions and something to consider for sure, but before we do that, we must ask a better question. What do I believe I can accomplish? We only believe in our future what we think we are capable of doing. Most people don't know how to dream big, and believe those dreams are possible. We see what is going on around us, and we simply hope to maybe "out-do" the status quo by a little. A child growing up in a middle-class community might hope that he will keep the status quo for his life, or maybe increase it a little. Or that child may not have any hope of ever matching the economic status. **The way we see our future has a vital impact on how we determine to live our lives.**

If I just finish college? If I just get married? If I just could possibly buy a house? For some these might be tiny goals that seem easy and for others they are a huge pipe dream. But Why? Why is it a pipe dream to own a home and have a spouse? You are reading this right now and making judgements on your own dreams. Are they big enough? Are they God sized dreams? Can you see yourself "out-doing" the cultural norms of your community? We are not just talking of financial dreams. We were called by God for different purposes. We were designed by God to be creative, to build, to raise the standard, to wow the public.

Before you read any further I want you to write down your current dreams and vision for your life. Go ahead, I'll wait!

Now I want you to evaluate what you just wrote down. I want you to ask a couple of very significant questions. Are my dreams something I can accomplish? Why, or why not? On a scale of 1 to 10, 1 being "this is easy and will be done tomorrow," 5 being "I can accomplish this in due time," and 10 being "this is impossible, but would be totally awesome," rate your dreams. Some of our dreams should be reachable and doable with simple effort and planning. Others, should be beyond reach in this lifetime and two more, if we had them. If there was a proper balance for how big your dreams are I would share it with you. But I will say this, if your average is below a 7 your dreams are most likely too small. Don't lose heart at this point. Understand that one is in the majority if their average score is less than 5. As I said earlier, the way we see our future is vital. The enemy has deceived us by making us think that we are in this alone, and that we are weak and frail and destined to fail. This is a big lie. You are not destined to fail. You were designed by God to not only succeed, but take the

> **You were designed by God to not only succeed, but take the enemies territory in the process**

enemies territory in the process. The devil knows that, so his goal is to keep you from believing it.

Psalms 139 tells us that God had a plan for our lives before time as we know it began. His plan is well thought out and perfect in every way. It's as if He wrote the story of our lives in a book. Each and every day of your life was pre-recorded by God and your story is epic. Because He created you, and knows you better than you know yourself, He was able to plan the days the way you would love them according to your strengths and abilities. Jeremiah 29:11 reminds us that His plans are to prosper us and give us a hope and a future, not to harm us. There are hundreds of verses about our defeating the enemy and living victorious.

*John 16:33 I have told you all this so that you may have peace in me. Here on earth you will have many trials and sorrows. But take heart, because I have **overcome** the world."*

*Isaiah 41:10 Don't be afraid, for I am with you. Don't be discouraged, for I am your God. I will strengthen you and help you. I will hold you up with my **victorious** right hand.*

Before we can really learn to dream big, we must come to the conclusion and believe that God is good, and He wants us to be successful. He created you and planned that you would be successful. It's already in that book of His. I never dreamed as a child growing up in the church that God would use me to travel the world and preach His gospel, or write books, or even influence thousands of students as their pastor. To me those were not even on my list. I didn't understand that God wanted to use me and that it would be awesome. I was too worried about money and the lack of it. I was saturated in self-doubt. I wasn't the business type, I didn't really like school and I didn't see a way of making big money. What I didn't see is that God didn't need me to be those things, He created me to love people and lead them. He created me to speak truth into people who were trapped in the lies of the enemy. He called me to set others free. First, He had to set me free from wrong thinking. He had to illuminate the truth to me. I am just beginning to learn how big I can dream. How far will God take me? How far will God take you? What is written in that story book of His? I'll get back to that story book later in this chapter.

Without a vision for the future, without a hope, without a dream, life does not have any meaning. Without a vision, we can retreat into a death spiral that takes us down the road from being blah and lifeless

Without a vision for the future, without a hope, without a dream, life does not have any meaning.

to full depression. It is a self-defeating prophecy. We think we do not have much to offer and no vision to work towards, so we back off. We stop trying. We hide. Our work ethic starts to suffer, our relationships can become unhealthy, and we become lazy. The thought that life has no hope, is now starting to become reality all because of our thought process. Pr. 6, along with many other verses warns of laziness. Laziness is seen in the way we live. It affects our work, our relationships, and even our health. Laziness is the after-effect of the way we see life. Laziness is a spiritual problem. When we do not see the glorious future that the Father has already written for us, it is a problem. We don't have to see it page by page but we should see and agree with the fact that He is good and desires good things for us. If we don't, then we have a spiritual problem. It's really a simple problem that is easy to fix. Heb. 12:2 tells us to fix our eyes on Jesus the author and finisher of our faith. This is repentance at its best, when we take our eyes and fix them on Jesus. Repentance is going from wrong thinking away from Jesus, to fixing our eyes on Him and allowing Him to be our focal point. He is the author of our story. Our biggest goal and greatest dream is to simply live out the magnitude of the story that He wrote for us.

Depression lacks vision! Depression is a state of mind that has little or no hope. Having no hope is to have your mind apart from the will of God for your life. Romans 12b *"be transformed by the renewing of your mind, so that you may prove what the will of God is, that which is good and acceptable and perfect"*. God's will is not just good, it's not just acceptable, it is perfect. Dream of a life that is perfect and that would just be a starting point. God's thoughts are higher than ours. Our perfection is limited but His is unlimited. His perfection is beyond our imagination. So if God's will for your life is perfect beyond your imagination, then depression is a lie. The emotions that we call depression are based on lies. Maybe one huge lie, maybe a series of lies, maybe a life built upon lies, but lies none the less. We must learn to replace the lie with the truth that God is good beyond measure. From there we can begin to dream again of a vibrant victorious future. We can begin to see ourselves in the story that God himself wrote before time began. We can begin to see ourselves for who we truly are. The key is that we begin to see! Vision!

Allow yourself to see God's story of you and dream big. Allow yourself to dream with God. Allow yourself to dream God-size dreams. And believe that all things are not only possible but probable in Jesus. He is the one who gave you the desires of your heart. He designed and created you to fulfill dreams that were according to your personality and likeness. He created you and

> **Repentance is going from wrong thinking away from Jesus, to fixing our eyes on Him and allowing Him to be our focal**

gifted you with the ability to fulfill His story of you. Some people call it your destiny. Some may call it your calling. Either way, the only way to fulfill your destiny or calling is to dream big and believe that all of God's promises are yes and AMEN.

*2 Cor. 1:20 For as many as are the promises of God, in Him they are **yes**; therefore also through Him is our **Amen** to the glory of God through us.*

Now let's take this a step further and speak of the rewards that God has for you.

*2 John 1:8 Watch out that you do not lose what we have worked so hard to achieve. Be diligent so that you receive your **full** reward.*

I put the word "full" in bold print because it is a descriptive word. It makes it clear that if we are to receive a "full" reward, then there is a possibility of only receiving a partial or no reward. That's right, there are rewards that God has for us and they could be anything from a gumball to reigning and ruling in His Kingdom. Paul said that He had finished the race, that he had remained faithful. How did Paul know that he had finished? During my college years, I was trying out for the soccer team and we had to run five miles under a certain time. It felt like a sprint for me. I tried to quit at one point feeling I could not run one more step. A friend grabbed me by the back of the shirt and drug me until I committed to finishing. When I crossed the finish line, it was a feeling like no other. Exhausted, exhilarated and triumphant all at the same time. I had finished with a few seconds to spare. I had finished the race. That's easy to look at because it is a simple task, run fast and finish on time. But life is so much more. The Bible says that we will be judged for not only our words but our thoughts and motives as well. How can I lay on my deathbed and know that I have finished the race, that I have kept the faith? I will keep the answer simple. Remember I said in a previous chapter that it has nothing to do with performance. It doesn't even matter if I finished the race under a certain time. If I dreamed big, if I went after the desires of my heart, if I sought God and His plan for my life, then I will hear him say something like, "well done, my good and faithful servant, enter now into your rest and receive your full reward."

That little boy playing with his firetruck is where God wants us to be: Free from fear; free from worry; free from self-doubt; free from feeling inadequate. You are more than capable. You were designed by God to accomplish more than you can dream. You were created to be creative, to build, to raise the standard.

The story of your life is an epic tale, the kind we pay money to see acted out on the big screen. Yes, it will have challenges. Yes, it will have triumphs. Yes, it will have a variety of emotions and unknowns in the future. But we know this. Your life is blessed and ordained by the Creator Himself to be Glorious. It is promised to be a life full of passion, and victory. It is promised to be a life full of His presence. It is the presence of God that empowers us to live above and beyond our circumstances. It is the presence of God that helps us understand what it means to live as God lives. Your story was written with the partnership of you and God working together for the greater good of mankind. That's epic!

Eph. 3:19. . . and to know the love of Christ which surpasses knowledge, that you may be filled up to all the fullness of God.

Now, stop and align your thoughts with God's. Ask Him to show you a glimpse of the greatness of His Glory for your life. Ask Him to increase your vision, to increase your hope, to increase your faith. Ask Him to help you dream His dreams. They are bigger than you think. DREAM BIG!

10   Spirit of Offense

*"If another believer sins against you, go privately and point out the **offense**. If the other person listens and confesses it, you have won that person back.*

One day I had been with a friend for a while and it was time to leave. As he headed to the door I graciously told him to "have a good day". I was shocked when his reply was, "don't tell me how to spend my day". Yes, he was kidding but it caused me to think about how sensitive we are to the responses or attitudes of others.

Let me tell you a half true story that will illustrate my point. Once upon a time there was a woman in a church that had a great heart and was always willing to serve and help whenever needed. She was middle aged, but took good care of herself and some would say that she was attractive. The whole church knew of her because she was quite flamboyant during worship. She sat in the front and was not afraid to express herself with clapping her hands or even dancing a little. She had a great smile and a joyful disposition. She was a single mom of two grown sons who were not near home. She naturally missed them, and because they were not following Jesus, she found comfort in helping other young men as if they were her own. I can assure you that her heart was pure, but as you can imagine, others questioned her motives in serving/helping younger men. She was not afraid to give them a hug or pray for them in public. Well, as it goes in the church, some thought it was inappropriate for her to pray for, or hug young men, and they even began to use words like flirtatious. One even called her a "cougar." (a term used when older women prey on young men)

As you read this you are already coming up with your own judgment based on the evidence that I have presented to you. Your

> **If your opinion of yourself differs from God's, then your opinion needs to be changed.**

background in church, home, school or culture helps shape your judgment. If this were you, and you knew you were innocent of all malice and sinful thought, you might get offended at being called a cougar for encouraging and praying for others. One may be in the middle thinking, it sounds questionable. And others are already accusing in their hearts that she is guilty of sin. We know that the Bible says, "Do not judge." It is almost as if we should defend ourselves by judging others because they are judging us. That is the kind of thought that gets us in a lot of trouble. That is the spirit of offense.

It can be very easy to get offended. But what at are we really getting offended? If you stop and look at this situation from a non-partisan perspective, you can see that this girl is being judged based on what others see in her character. Only God knows her true heart and motives. The only thing to get offended in this situation is someone else's false judgement. I say false judgment because no one really knows. The truth is we love to make judgements based on what we see and hear, but are we correct? Is it wise to let someone's opinion cause us to get offended? We have a hard enough time keeping control of our own thoughts, why are we being offended by another's opinion? That's exactly at what we are looking, someone's opinion.

I cannot control how anyone thinks. I cannot control the thoughts or emotions of anyone else, but my own. If I let the thoughts and emotions of others offend me, then I am the one that is going to be emotionally unstable. One day you are on an emotional

> **If the devil, can get you to look at your own flaws, then your mind will no longer line up with God's because He sees you as perfect in every way.**

high because someone said you looked good, but the next day you heard a comment that your clothes are out of style. Everyone has an opinion, usually about everything. Let me ask you a very important question. **What does it matter what someone thinks about you?** If it is someone close to you, and they have an opinion, it is wise to listen and see if their remark is worth considering. But a stranger, who does not have your best interest in mind, let it go. We should be very careful whom we allow to speak into our lives. When others speak, we get to give permission to whom we will listen.

Let me say this with all the kindness in my heart, "Stop"! Everyone around you has some opinion of you. Do you want to know what they all are, NO. My instruction to you is for you to practice letting offensive comments or thoughts just roll off your back. The only opinion that matters is God's. He has already said throughout His Word that He loves you and adores you. God's thoughts for you are amazing and too numerous to count (Psalm 40:5). If your opinion of yourself differs from God's, then your opinion needs to be changed. Bill Johnson from Bethel Church in Redding says, "I can't afford to have a thought about me in my head that He (God) doesn't have in His head about me." If I entertain thoughts about me that are not absolutely true and central in His perspective about me, then I'm entertaining thoughts that will war against what He thinks about me." Our thoughts need to line up with His thoughts or we are agreeing with the enemy. In other words, we are at war with God in our thoughts because we are agreeing with the enemy of God. Listening and entertaining thoughts from others, that don't line up with the Father is a bad habit that must be broken.

The devil has been laying this trap from the very beginning. He is poking fingers at our pride, or what some would call our ego. The only part of us that can be offended is our pride which Proverbs tells us it is wise to get rid of. If someone says something about me or thinks something about me that does not line up with who I am in Christ, then I have no reason to get offended because it is wrong. If I do get offended, it is because I am thinking with the carnal mind, which is my pride. It is my pride therefore that has been hurt. There is no other part of me that can be emotionally hurt.   The devil's plan is to divide and conquer. He started in the garden when he spoke to Eve and said, "*Did God really say...?*" He is a liar and called the accuser of the brethren. According to Rev. 12:10, the enemy stands between you and God and accuses you. His goal is to get your eyes off the Lord and on your problems. Accusations are what we are talking about. If you let them, other people's opinions become accusations. It is the devil's plan for you to stop looking to God and to get you to look at your flaws, or even the flaws of others. Because, after all it sure feels better to look at someone else's flaws rather

> **We would not be judgmental to others if were not critical of ourselves, and we would not be critical of ourselves if we kept our mind on the truth of who we are in Christ in the first place.**

than our own. If the devil can get you to look at your own flaws, then your mind will no longer line up with God's, because He sees you as perfect in every way. Stop right there and thank God for the way he sees you, PERFECT! Looking at your flaws gets old and frustrating right away, so we start looking to others and their faults. We become judgmental because it makes us feel better about ourselves. We would not be judgmental to others if were not critical of ourselves, and we would not be critical of ourselves if we kept our mind on the truth of who we are in Christ in the first place.

Look at social media for just a few minutes and you will see the two sides of every issue. It happens in politics, it happens in culture, and it happens in the church. It is impossible to escape the judgment of others. We have been raised on different levels of racism and denominationalism. On the political side the left mocks the right and vice versa. In the church, the Baptist think the Pentecostals are out of their mind. We all have our differences, and I am not writing here to settle the sides. I am writing to expose the devil's plan to separate us from the love of God. We must learn to not let others offend us. Our goal should be to see ourselves and others as God sees us. I don't have to agree with someone to love them. If I see them from my natural eyes, I see faults and differences, and I won't like what I see. But when I see them from Spiritual eyes, I am able to see them as God sees them.

The Bible makes it clear that our battle is not against flesh and blood, but against the devil and his schemes (Eph. 6:12). When are we going to learn this lesson? When are we going to figure out that the devil has a plan and every time we get offended at another person, we have just fallen prey to his plan. He lies, he lies, he lies, and then he lies some more while pushing your buttons. He attacks in so many ways. Whatever has offended you in the past, be sure that he is going to use the same tactic unless you stop him. Why should he change his attack, when we make it so easy for him? We should not get offended at the person who made the remark or acted in a specific way. We should recognize that, "the devil made him do it." Okay, maybe the devil didn't make them do it, but it was his idea and his suggestion. Our battle is not against the person but against the spirit that is influencing that person.

There is a great little book that I highly suggest by Steve Backland called, "let's just laugh at that." It suggests that we learn to laugh at all the lies that we now know are truth. For instance, if you hear a lie that you are unworthy, you could get offended, hurt, angry and you could believe that you are unworthy. But we know that it is a lie. Christ has made you worthy by His death and resurrection. He has declared that you are worthy to be in His presence. So, let's just laugh at the lie. Don't just chuckle or laugh to yourself, laugh out loud and laugh hard. Laugh at yourself for believing the lie in the first place. Yes, it's ok to laugh at yourself. It's actually quite freeing to be able to laugh at your past mistakes. It is a sign that your pride is being laid down, and that you are no longer offended at yourself.

If we allow ourselves, we can be offended at the clothes others wear. I was at a church once where a teenage girl was dressed a little less than others thought comfortable and so they made her wear a very large ugly shirt while she was there (if anyone had a right to be offended it was her). Or we can very easily be offended by the profane words others use. As a pastor, I could be offended because one does not like the way I run the church service. What if someone is rude to you? What if someone is not thankful when they should be? What if someone does not pay back when they should? What if someone cuts you off on the freeway while giving you an obscene gesture? What if someone you care about says something negative about you? What I want you to understand is that there is nothing you can do to control the actions of others. You cannot control what their day has been like. You cannot control how others have treated them prior to your encounter with them. Maybe they are beyond stressed, maybe they had just heard bad news, and maybe they are just exhausted and not thinking clearly... You get my point. I am not making excuses for others' behavior, I'm just making it clear that the actions and words of others should not affect your emotions.

The woman at the church ministering to the young men should not allow the judgments of others to affect her emotions. She is a child of the Lord and accountable to Him. But at the same time we are supposed to avoid the appearance of evil because we don't want to cause weaker believers to stumble. I purposely do my best to avoid situations where others might be offended, not because I care what they think, but because I am trying to lead them towards Christ and not cause them to stumble. When a situation comes up where one might get offended, it is a good time to stop and analyze what the truth is. Does the accusing or negative party have a point? Is there something I should or could do differently that would help? Am I honoring God with my actions and words?

> **It's actually quite freeing to be able to laugh at your past mistakes. It is a sign that your pride is being laid down, and that you are no longer offended at yourself.**

What to do if offended by a friend.

It is not wrong to confront a brother when they do or say something that is offensive. The problems arise when we confront without love. Every relationship has its hard times, and usually it is something small that gets escalated to something larger. A husband didn't take out the trash, so the wife gets mad and calls him lazy. Maybe he was being lazy at the moment, and maybe she had a bad day. It doesn't matter. Once a derogatory name has been called, it's on. Now he calls her a nag; then she feels unloved and unappreciated so says something about how bad a husband and father he is, and so it goes. STOP! No one wants to be called a name. It never helps! No one wants to be treated with discontent! The universal golden rule is to treat others how you want to be treated. We usually don't do that when we are responding out of hurt or anger. Maybe the wife could have said, "Honey, the trash in the kitchen is starting to smell and is overflowing, is there a time soon when you will be able to take it out for me? I would really appreciate it." Then he, the husband, if he was smart and kind, would get up and take care of it ASAP. Silly example, I know, but the simple things can really get out of hand if we let them. Confronting with love is the key. If the words that come from your mouth are not seasoned with love, then hold them back. The enemy wants to use your words to offend others whenever possible; don't give him the opportunity.

Now that you know the truth, it's easy to see that the spirit of offense is a tactical maneuver of the enemy to steal, kill and destroy our lives. I want to give you some practical ways to avoid being offended.

1. **Know your true identity**. God loves you and adores you. He has redeemed you and called you his own. You are God's and He has your back. He has a plan to prosper you and give you a hope and a future. You are royalty in the Kingdom of God. This whole book is about what Christ has done to set you free from bondage of lies and oppression. Keep learning who you are. Every promise in the Bible to you is still valid and God is incapable of breaking them. He will fulfill what He has promised.

2. **Realize that others don't usually mean to be offensive**. It is human nature to defend ourselves. Not all the time, but usually, when a person says or does something that is offensive to you, they didn't mean it. Have you ever said something you wish you could take back? Understanding this will help one not to rush to judgment and speak negatively in return. This is a great time to confront with love. Lovingly one can say, "When you said those words, what did you mean by them?"

3. **Don't let others determine your value**. If God says you are special, who do you allow to say otherwise? You are valuable even if you don't feel like you are. Remember that emotions follow your thinking. Believe that you are valuable and soon you will start feeling like you are worthy. The Bible says that no weapon formed against us shall prosper. Don't let lies, or the negative opinions of others speak to your identity.

4. **Declare the truth out loud**. The power of life and death are in the tongue. Use your own tongue to speak life over yourself. Declare that you are worthy. Declare that you are valuable. Whenever a lie tries to sneak its way into your

mind, declare the opposite out loud. The enemy does not know what you are thinking unless you tell him. He can read the expressions on your face or hear your words, but he is not a mind reader. He lies and then waits for a response from you. If you respond with declarations of truth over your life, proclaiming the name of Jesus as your Savior and King, he will leave. The Bible says to resist the devil and he will flee from you. Declare truth and watch him run.

5. **Declare your love for yourself.** This is so important. It is not egotistical or self-centered to love yourself. It is to line your thoughts up with God's. It is to understand that you are a beloved child of God that is worth loving because of Christ and the finished work of the cross. You are fearfully and wonderfully made in the image of God. If He loves you enough to send His Son Jesus to die for you, then you must be worth loving. He is love, all that He loves is lovable. Therefore, you are lovable. Love yourself well!

6. **Kill your pride.** Pride cannot live if you want to be joyful. Pride is an inward focus on yourself. There is no joy in the worthless self apart from Christ. If I look at myself without

Jesus, I see faults, faults, and more faults. I try to cover them up with my abilities and accomplishments, but in the end, I will be empty. If you have killed your pride then you can't get hurt or offended because there is nothing to get hurt. It is already dead! When you realize that all of your value comes from Christ and His redemption, it makes it easy to lay all your pride down. Jack Hayford (Author and pastor of Church on the Way), tells a story about a person in his congregation who approached him with a suggestion. She suggested that during worship they tone down the encouragement to lift hands to the Lord because it might be uncomfortable for the visitors, it might offend their pride. His response was, "I'm not trying to offend their pride, I'm trying to kill it".

7. **Thanksgiving and praise!** Read the last chapter!

11 Praise and Thanksgiving

Psalm 100: 4 Enter His gates with thanksgiving and His courts with praise; give thanks to him and praise his name.

"Don't reduce God to the size of your emotions".
Roger Gales

Wisdom is something to behold. Wisdom is not street smarts or head knowledge. I know many people who have advanced degrees but are not very wise. I have friends that know the Bible inside and out, but have a hard time understanding who God is and what He wants from us. James 1 tells us to ask for wisdom. When I was in the upper half of my twenties, I met a young pastor, Dan Atchison, who was so full of wisdom, I was magnetically drawn to him. He told me that he had been trained since he was young to ask for wisdom. Not just a little wisdom but wisdom of the elderly who knew Jesus well. I saw the fulfillment of James 1 in front of my eyes. Needless to say, I began asking for the same thing.

Proverbs 4:7 Getting wisdom is the wisest thing you can do! And whatever else you do, develop good judgment. 8 If you prize wisdom, she will make you great. Embrace her, and she will honor you. 9 She will place a lovely wreath on your head; she will present you with a beautiful crown."

I have a spiritual son who is an amazing man of God. When he was in high school he had a crush on a beautiful young lady, who lived in another county. Nothing ever came of it until they were both in their young twenties. She came to live with my family in Arizona so that she could go to school. He came out to visit and they hit it off. It was not long before they became engaged and Cristian was beside himself with joy as he drove home to the mountains of California. Two weeks later he decided to make an impromptu trip see her again. He had not been able to reach her by phone for few days, so he figured he needed to come. When he got there, it was not good. She had decided that being engaged to him was not what she wanted, and he was heartbroken. I was so heartbroken for both of them. What we witnessed next was a great example for all to follow. In his brokenness, Cristian displayed more wisdom and honor than I have ever seen to this day. He grabbed his guitar, went to a place of solitude, and he worshipped the Lord. He worshipped well into the morning. There was weeping in the midst of the worship, but it was authentic worship. He knew that there is no greater place of joy, love, comfort and compassion than the presence of the Lord.

Col. 1:10-12 . . . that you will walk in a manner worthy of the Lord, to please Him in all respects, bearing fruit in every good work and increasing in the knowledge of God; 11 strengthened with all power, according to His glorious might, for the attaining of all steadfastness and patience; joyously [12] *giving thanks to the Father, who has qualified us to share in the inheritance of the saints in Light.*

This is where I want to leave you. **In His Presence**.

Life is a series of happenings. Some are fun and exhilarating while others are hard and miserable. If I allow my surroundings to dictate my level of joy, I will forever be on an emotional rollercoaster. Stress, worry, anxiety, fear and depression are all the result of an emotional rollercoaster that went off track. Thankfulness expressed, is the antidote for worry and stress. Thankfulness is a choice. There is always something for which to be thankful. If you have a relationship with Jesus, you have to be thankful for Him. Be purposeful, and fight hard to be thankful when it does not seem possible. Psalm 100 tells us to enter His gates with thanksgiving in your heart. Proverbs 4:23 also tells us to guard our heart, because it determines the course of our life. Relationships are not at home in the mind, they reside in the heart. In your heart, you can choose to enter into His presence with thankfulness even in the most difficult circumstances. If it helps you, write out a list of all the things for which you are thankful. When your mind has control and won't allow you to be thankful, get the list out and read it out loud over and over.

Phil. 4:8 Finally, brethren, whatever is true, whatever is honorable, whatever is right, whatever is pure, whatever is lovely, whatever is of good repute, if there is any excellence and if anything worthy of praise, dwell on these things. 9 The things you have learned and received and heard and seen in me, practice these things, and the God of peace will be with you.

You get to choose what you think about. Your thoughts are determined by you. They are real, but they are not always correct. You can choose to see the best in people or their faults. You can choose to see the best (Jesus) in you or not. But we must come to realize that our feelings (emotions) follow our thinking. We are what we focus our thoughts on.

Pr. 23:7 As a man thinks, so he is.

It would benefit us to learn to think according to the promises of God. It is His promises, that when fully grasped, allows us to share in His divine nature (2 Pet 1:3, 4). Our mental health depends on it.

We are told to take every thought captive to the obedience of Christ. That means we must rid ourselves of wrong thoughts and practice thinking according to the thoughts of God. Worship God, regardless of the happenings around you. Worship God regardless of the situation you are in. It is God's desire that we worship Him. We were created to worship Him. Now before one goes off thinking that God is an egoist and needs our worship, one must understand that everything God does is motivated by love. It is God's desire that we become like Jesus. Here is some really great news. You become like that which you worship. In God's wisdom, He knew that if we turned our affections on Him and worshipped Him, we would become like Him. We are learning to see with our spiritual eyes. To remove the lies of the enemy that sit like a veil in front of our eyes.

2 Cor. 3:18 . . . all of us who have had that veil removed can see and reflect the glory of the Lord. And the Lord—who is the Spirit—makes us more and more like him as we are changed into his glorious image. The more we know about God the better. But, as we worship Him, we become like Him. We will continue to get to know Him better as time goes on. And the more I know of Him the more I want to worship Him because He is so good and so worthy of Praise. Judson

Cornwall said, "We are transformed in proportion to the time spent in the Glory and Presence of Jesus". Whoa! Do I need to say that again? The more time with Jesus, the more I am transformed. Drop the mic!

The more we know Him, the more we can trust in Him because we learn that He is trustworthy.

> **Thankfulness will pull you out of a mental funk, but praise will take you into a place of joy.**

Psalm 115:9-11 O Israel, trust in the LORD; He is their help and their shield. 10 O house of Aaron, trust in the LORD; He is their help and their shield. 11 You who fear the LORD, trust in the LORD; He is their help and their shield.

Prov 3:5,6 Trust in the Lord with your whole heart and lean not on your own understanding. In all your ways, acknowledge Him and He will make your paths straight.

Worship is declaring your trust in the Lord. If I am declaring my trust in the Lord, then I am also declaring that the situation that has me emotionally under the weather, has no power over me. The Bible tells us that God inhabits the praises of His people. In other words,

His presence, which is always with us, increases as we worship. When we are in the presence of the Prince of Peace, it is virtually impossible to be worried or stressed. When we are in the presence of love (God is Love), it is impossible to be depressed.

We are not to stop at being thankful. Enter His courts with thanksgiving and enter His courts with praise. We thank God for what He has done and we praise Him for who He is.

Pslam 48:1 Great is the Lord and greatly to be praised!

Thankfulness will pull you out of a mental funk, but praise will take you into a place of joy.

Thankfulness takes us from thinking of our problems, faults, and worries and puts them on the things of God. That is a great thing to do because our emotions will soon follow as they always do. Then we begin to praise the King of Kings and Lord of Lords and our thoughts are taken to another realm of His glory. It is in the Glory of the Lord that true joy is present.

*2 Cor. 3:18 But we all, with unveiled face, beholding as in a mirror the **glory** of the Lord, are being transformed into the same image from **glory to glory**, just as from the Lord, the Spirit.*

The purpose of worship is to take us to deeper levels of glory. God wants us to become more like Him. He is love! He is joy! He is peace. Romans tells us that the Kingdom of God is righteousness, peace, and joy. We know that in Heaven there is no sadness, depression, worry, anxiety or fear. We become like that which we worship. For some it has been years of worry and stress, maybe even deep depression. The definition of insanity is to do the same thing over and over again expecting different results. The enemy has lied to us for so long and we have been stuck in the insanity of "lack" for way too long. We are not lacking anything, we have just thought that we lacked. It's time to make a change. To do something different. To change the outcome, we must change the method. We must turn our thoughts to Jesus, the author and finisher of our faith. We must fight through the negativity that the enemy is bombarding us with and start declaring, out loud, the goodness of God. We must not fight for truth, we must fight from truth. The truth of God will set us free. We must not fight for freedom, we must fight from freedom.

*Gal 5:1 It was for **freedom** that Christ set us free; therefore keep standing firm and do not be subject again to a yoke of slavery*

We have can have freedom from negative emotions and the sicknesses and diseases that come with them. We can have freedom from worry, anxiety, fear and depression. They are all forms of slavery. Our thoughts can enslave us or set us free. We must change our thoughts if we want to change the outcome. We must change our thoughts if we want to be free. Christ has already paved the way, given us an example, and broken the curse of sin. We must simply believe, and be set free.

Worship accomplishes so many things. Ps. 22 tells us that God is enthroned upon the praises of His people. When we worship, we are establishing God's rightful place in our lives. He is Lord and master of our lives. We exalt Him to that place of honor and Lordship where He belongs. As we have already learned, worship changes the worshipper. It makes us more like Him taking us from Glory to Glory. Worship also changes the atmosphere. Even one person worshipping can change the atmosphere in a room. But when many gather to worship, there is an atmospheric shift into His presence.

2 Chr. 5:13. . . in unison when the trumpeters and the singers were to

make themselves heard with one voice to praise and to glorify

the LORD, and when they lifted up their voice accompanied by trumpets

and cymbals and instruments of music, and when they praised

the LORD saying, "He indeed is good for His lovingkindness is

everlasting," then the house, the house of the LORD, was filled with

a cloud.

I have walked into a room where the worship has ended but there is

still a powerful presence of the Lord that is lingering. It is a

wonderful place to be in the presence of the Lord.   Worship invites a

more powerful presence of the Lord. We know God will never leave

us nor forsake us, so in a sense, His presence is always with us.

Hebrews 4 says that nothing can be hidden from His presence. But

then John 15 tells us to remain in His abiding presence.

John 15:4- 8 ⁴Abide in Me, and I in you. As the branch cannot bear

fruit of itself unless it abides in the vine, so neither can you unless you

abide in Me. ⁵I am the vine, you are the branches; he who abides in Me

and I in him, he bears much fruit, for apart from Me you can do

nothing. ⁶If anyone does not abide in Me, he is thrown away as a

branch and dries up; and they gather them, and cast them into the fire and they are burned. 7 If you abide in Me, and My words abide in you, ask whatever you wish, and it will be done for you. 8 My Father is glorified by this, that you bear much fruit, and so prove to be My disciples.

He is always with us but He encourages us to abide in His presence. That is a conscious choice for us be in a deeper level of His presence.

> **He created you and called you to partner with Him in defeating the enemy, and taking back authority of the earth and all that it contains**

Then there is even a deeper level. *Acts 1:8 but you will receive power when the **Holy Spirit** has come upon you; and you shall be My witnesses both in Jerusalem, and in all Judea and Samaria, and even to the remotest part of the earth."*

This is the mighty presence of God where we get to partner with Him to accomplish all that he has set before us. God did not create you just to get by in life. He created you and called you to partner with Him in defeating the enemy, and taking back authority of the earth and all that it contains. The Holy Spirit is in you to guide you and strengthen you. He is in you to comfort you and reveal the things of God to you.

But then He is there to empower you to go beyond the natural. When we are baptized in the Holy Spirit, we are empowered to do everything that God has set before us. That includes preaching, teaching, loving others, healing physical and emotional sickness, giving sight to the blind and even raising the dead. Worship delights the Father. Psalm 134 tells us that the Lord takes pleasure in His people. But more than anything worship accomplishes spiritual warfare.

Ps 8:2 From the mouth of infants and nursing babes You have established strength,   because of Your adversaries, To make the enemy and the revengeful cease.

The battle for your mind is at hand. You are a redeemed child of God, full of the Holy Spirit and power. You were created to worship and become like the one you worship, full of love and joy. The Bible reminds us who the winner is. Jesus wins! We are on His side. We are on the winning side. One day we will stand next to Jesus and see Him face to face and all will be done. There will be no more sadness, no more sickness, no more pain. The question is, what about now. How will we do in the battles until then? The battle for your joy is between your ears. How will we do? We know that we win in the end. We know that God has made a way, He has made us right with Him already. We know that the enemy is a liar and a thief who has already been defeated. Fight the battle for truth now. The truth will set you free. Worry, stress, anxiety, fear, and depression have no place in the Kingdom and they have no place in our lives. Stop them, defeat them, kill them!

www.ingramcontent.com/pod-product-compliance
Lightning Source LLC
LaVergne TN
LVHW051234080426
835513LV00016B/1570